5/10

FOSSIL RIDGE PUBLIC LIBRARY DISTRICT

W9-BTQ-806

World War II: Essential Histories

World War II

Northwest Europe 1944–1945

Robert O'Neill, Series Editor; Russell Hart and Stephen Hart

ROSEN
PUBLISHING®

New York

Fossil Ridge Public Library District
Braidwood, IL 60408

--This edition published in 2010 by:

The Rosen Publishing Group, Inc.
29 East 21st Street
New York, NY 10010

Additional end matter copyright © 2010 by The Rosen Publishing Group, Inc.

All rights reserved. No part of this publication may be reproduced, stored in a retrieval system or transmitted in any form or by any means, without the prior written consent of the publisher.

Library of Congress Cataloging-in-Publication Data

O'Neill, Robert John.
World War II: Northwest Europe, 1944–1945 / Robert O'Neill, Russell Hart, and Stephen Hart.
    p. cm.—(World War II: essential histories)
Includes bibliographical references and index.
ISBN 978-1-4358-9129-6 (library binding)
1. World War, 1939–1945—Campaigns—Western Front—Juvenile literature. I. Hart, R. (Russell) II. Hart, S. (Stephen), 1968– III. Title.
D756.O545 2010
940.54'21—dc22

2009025523

Manufactured in Malaysia

CPSIA Compliance Information: Batch #TW10YA: For Further Information contact Rosen Publishing, New York, New York at 1-800-237-9932

Copyright © 2002 Osprey Publishing Limited. First published in paperback by Osprey Publishing Limited.

On the cover: American soldiers landing in France from the ramp of a Coast Guard landing boat, June 6, 1944. (NARA 26-G-2343)

Contents

Introduction

The Northwest Europe campaign was the decisive military operation conducted by the Western Allies in the European theater during World War II. This global conflict, the largest and most devastating war in human history, broke out in September 1939 as a result of Hitler's racist plan for global domination by an ethnically cleansed Third Reich that would endure for a millennium. During 1939–41, Hitler's Nazi war machine overran continental Europe and the Führer's plans for world domination culminated with Operation Barbarossa – his June 22, 1941 genocidal onslaught against the Soviet Union. This total war aimed to destroy both the Soviet Union and Communism, and to enslave the Slavic Soviet peoples for the benefit of the Aryan master race.

On December 10, 1941, Hitler compounded the folly of attacking the Soviet Union by declaring war on the USA in response to the surprise Japanese attack against Pearl Harbor. In the meantime, Great Britain stood alone against Germany, fighting a war of widely fluctuating fortunes in North Africa and the Middle East during 1940–42. During 1943 the tide of war finally turned as the Western Allies took the offensive in the Mediterranean and the Soviets drove back the Germans in the east.

The Northwest Europe campaign witnessed the return to western Europe of American, British, and Commonwealth forces, as well as contingents drawn from the European countries occupied by Nazi Germany. In the D-Day landings on June 6, 1944, the Western Allies fought their way ashore in the face of strong enemy resistance and established a bridgehead in Normandy. Allied forces repulsed all German efforts to overrun the bridgehead, then assumed the offensive and captured the port of Cherbourg, crucial for the long-term viability of the lodgment, by the end of June. Thereafter, in a series of bitter battles, the Allies first captured the key cities of Caen and St. Lô.

In late July, after many weeks of grim attritional warfare, the Americans finally broke out of the Normandy bridgehead. Aided by supporting landings on the French Mediterranean coast in mid-August, the Allies swept through France, pushed into Belgium and in early September captured the key port of Antwerp. But during September 8–12 the German defense regained coherence in northern Belgium and in front of Germany's western frontier. It took hard, brutal attritional battles to advance to the German West Wall defenses amid autumn mud and rain. While the Allies achieved several local penetrations of the West Wall, nowhere were they able to punch through the full depth of the German fortifications and achieve operational success.

During mid-December a major German counteroffensive in the Ardennes drove the Americans back in the thinly held Schnee Eifel, but fell far short of its overambitious goal of recapturing Antwerp and thus splitting the Allied front. The Germans followed up this partial success with an even less successful offensive in Alsace; and both offensives simply dissipated Germany's meager reserves of troops, weaponry, and supplies. Hard-fought Allied attacks finally broke through the West Wall during the late winter and drove the Germans back to the Rhine on a broad front.

With the arrival of spring, the Allies launched their final offensives that shattered the German defenses along the Rhine River, and advanced through western Germany into central Germany to meet advancing Soviet forces on the Elbe at Torgau on April 25, 1945.

By this stage German resistance had disintegrated, and Western Allied forces swept through southwestern Germany and into Austria, while also advancing to the Elbe River on a broad front. Hitler committed suicide in Berlin on April 30 and Germany capitulated unconditionally on May 8, 1945, bringing to a close World War II in Europe.

Undoubtedly, without the Northwest Europe campaign World War II in Europe would have gone on much longer and thus the misery suffered by those languishing under harsh German occupation would have been the greater. Moreover, the postwar "Iron Curtain" dividing capitalist and Communist blocs would have been moved much farther west. For, in the long run, the Soviet Union – which bore the brunt of the fighting in the European theater – would have ground Germany into defeat. The Allied invasion of France, therefore, certainly speeded the demise of Hitler's Reich, which thus endured for only 12 – rather than 1,000 – years. Despite the Anglo-American command disputes that accompanied the campaign, this multinational effort also helped to reinforce the idea of a "special relationship" between the USA and Great Britain, that, some would say, continues to this day.

Chronology

1944 **June 6** D-Day landings
June 7 British capture Bayeux
June 10 Germans assume the defensive
June 14 Germans begin V1 rocket offensive on London
June 17 Americans break out across Cotentin peninsula
June 19–30 Battle for Cherbourg
June 26–27 Montgomery launches Operation Epsom
June 28–July 2 German counteroffensive by II SS Panzer Corps
July 1 Last German resistance ceases in the Cotentin peninsula
July 7 Controversial Caen raid by Allied heavy bombers
July 8 Anglo-Canadian Charnwood offensive begins
July 9 Fall of northern Caen and German retreat behind the Orne River
July 18 Anglo-Canadian Goodwood offensive begins
July 25 American Cobra offensive
July 28 British Bluecoat offensive
July 31 Crerar's First Canadian Army becomes operational
August 6–8 German Lüttich counteroffensive on Avranches
August 8 Canadian Operation Totalize launched
August 13 Eisenhower halts Patton's advance toward Falaise
August 14 Canadians initiate Operation Tractable
August 18 Patton resumes his advance from Alençon toward Falaise
August 19 Falaise pocket sealed; II SS Panzer Corps launches relief operation
August 20–22 Partial German breakout from the Falaise pocket

August 21–31 German strategic withdrawal behind the Seine
September 1 Eisenhower assumes position of Land Forces Commander from Montgomery
Early September German V2 rocket offensive begins
September 1–9 Allies advance headlong toward the German frontier
September 4 Antwerp captured
September 4–26 German retreat behind the Scheldt estuary
September 5–30 Subjugation of the Channel ports of Le Havre, Boulogne, and Calais
September 13 Battle for Aachen begins
September 17–26 Allied Operation Market-Garden fails to cross Lower Rhine at Arnhem
October 2–16 Canadian advance on South Beveland
October 6 Canadian Operation Switchback begins
October 16 Isolation of Walcheren begins
October 21 Fall of Aachen – Siegfried Line penetrated
October 26–27 German Meijel counterattack
November 1–7 Canadian Operation Infatuate captures Walcheren
November 3 Breskens pocket cleared
November 8–22 Patton's Third US Army captures Metz
November 13–23 6th US Army Group captures Strasbourg and advances to Upper Rhine
November 14 Second British Army clears
November 16 American advance against Siegfried Line bogs down in the Hürtgen Forest

December 4 Venlo salient

December 16–22 German counteroffensive in the Ardennes makes progress

December 18–26 Battle for Bastogne rages

December 23 Allied counterattacks in Ardennes begin

1945 January 16–26 British Blackcock offensive clears west bank of the Roer River

January 20 First French Army subdues

February 8 Anglo-Canadian Veritable offensive clears Reichswald Forest

February 9 Colmar pocket

February 23 American Grenade offensive across the Roer

March 8–10 German Army Group H withdraws behind the Rhine

March 7 American forces capture Rhine bridge intact at Remagen

March 8–24 American forces clear west bank of the Rhine

March 19 Hitler enacts a scorched earth policy

March 22 Americans cross the Rhine at Oppenheim

March 23 Montgomery launches Operation Plunder assault across the Rhine at Wesel

March 28 Second British Army breaks out from Wesel bridgehead

April 1 German Army Group B encircled in the Ruhr pocket

April 8 British establish bridgeheads across the Weser River

April 17 Resistance in the Ruhr pocket ceases

April 19 Allies capture Nuremberg

April 20 German forces in the Netherlands isolated

April 25 American and Soviet forces meet at Torgau on the Elbe River

May 4 American forces cross Brenner Pass and link up in northern Italy

May 8 German capitulation

The road to D-Day

World War II became inevitable after Hitler's democratic rise to power in Germany during 1933. It was simply a matter of time before he launched aggression, since his world-view – shaped by racist Social Darwinism, virulent anti-Semitism, and his own Great War trench-combat experiences – embraced warfare as the final arbiter of national evolution. For Hitler, history was the story of racial struggle in which only the fittest race would survive. He believed that an idealized German race of blond-haired, blue-eyed Aryan supermen – Hitler was neither – was destined for global dominance. To the Führer, therefore, what remained was simply when, and on what terms, a renewal of the Great War would emerge.

None of this, of course, was readily apparent to most western politicians in the 1930s. They strove amid the difficult conditions imposed by the Great Depression and the shackling legacies of World War I to compromise with Hitler. Circumstances initially forced Hitler to act cautiously – reoccupying the demilitarized Rhineland in 1936 and effecting *Anschluss* (unification) with Austria in spring 1938. Unfortunately, western leaders erred fundamentally in regarding Hitler as a nineteenth-century statesman whose nationalist aspirations could be accommodated through negotiation. This appeasement policy only encouraged Hitler's aggression, for it reinforced his preconceived notions of his enemies as weak and racially inferior.

British Prime Minister Neville Chamberlain – like many of Europe's leading statesmen – believed that Hitler was a man with whom he could "do business": in other words, that Hitler would be satisfied with modest concessions. After securing a settlement during the 1938 Munich Crisis, Chamberlain believed that he had secured "peace in our time." Yet Europe's leaders failed woefully to appreciate both the grandiose scale of Hitler's aggressive ambitions – nothing less than world domination – and his eagerness to resort to war to secure these objectives. (Ann Ronan Picture Library)

Hitler's success in acquiring the Sudetenland from Czechoslovakia in 1938 without recourse to war did not, as Chamberlain hoped, satiate the Führer's demands: on the contrary, it fueled the aggressive audacity of his subsequent foreign policy, with Hitler effectively repudiating the Munich Agreement in March 1939 when Germany annexed Bohemia-Moravia. (AKG Berlin)

Hitler was not to be appeased: in fact, he bitterly regretted the Munich Agreement of 1938, where Britain and France postponed a general European war by surrendering to the Reich the Sudetenland region of Czechoslovakia, with its significant German minority. Despite this stunning diplomatic triumph, Hitler rued not being able to unleash his as yet imperfect war machine on his neighbors.

A sea change in the ineffectual western response to German expansionism materialized in March 1939 when Hitler broke his Munich pledge that the Sudetenland would be the last of his territorial ambitions, and suddenly occupied the rest of Czechoslovakia. Denuded of the Sudetenland, which contained a large proportion of Czechoslovakia's frontier defenses, heavy industry, and natural resources, and still numbed by the Anglo-French betrayal at Munich, the Czechs offered no resistance. This blatant repudiation of the Munich accord angered western sentiment, and it was this shifting public opinion that prodded the reluctant British and French governments to jettison appeasement and shift to a deterrent policy against future German aggression.

Britain and France postured – reintroducing peacetime conscription and doubling Britain's Territorial Army – to give the appearance of meaning business. Clutching at straws, they unwisely made a public pledge to defend the territorial integrity of Poland, the next likely victim of Nazi bullying. Unfortunately, Germany separated Poland geographically from its new allies, which rendered this pledge incredible because there was no possible way for Britain and France to defend Poland. Hitler called the Anglo-French bluff: he did not believe they were prepared to go to war over Poland and, even if they did, he knew that they could do little to thwart his aggression.

The only viable Anglo-French strategic option to stop Hitler was to revive the 1907 Triple Alliance with Russia that had successfully thwarted German aggression during the Great War. Yet Russia was now the Soviet Union and deep-seated suspicion and hostility toward Communism prevented Britain and France from recreating the only alliance that might have stayed German aggression. Instead it was Hitler who concluded the Molotov–Ribbentrop Pact of nonaggression with the Soviet Union, paving the way for German conquest of Poland. In a secret protocol, Stalin agreed to join Germany in dismembering Poland. With this guarantee, Germany invaded Poland on September 1. Ensnared by their public pledges to defend Poland, first Britain, and then France, reluctantly declared war on Germany on September 3, 1939.

Yet militarily there was little the Western Allies could do but observe Germany and the Soviet Union conquer Poland. This was the so-called "Phoney War" when British bombers refrained from dropping bombs for fear of injuring civilians – ineffective targeting technology meant that the bombers had little chance of hitting their targets, anyway. The French meanwhile launched a half-hearted offensive into the Saar that crawled forward against minimal opposition and then inexplicably halted. At the same time, both nations frantically mobilized their economies and populations for war, endeavoring to overcome in a few months the deleterious effects of two decades of underfunding, military retrenchment, and cultural pacifism.

Predictably, neither nation was capable of furnishing a balanced military capable of withstanding Nazi aggression when the Germans finally struck in the west during May 1940. Germany had started rearmament several years before its opponents, and the Nazi totalitarian dictatorship had pushed massive rearmament and militarism at a rate unacceptable in the democratic West. Moreover, and this was the crucial advantage, the Germans had gained considerable operational experiences from the military actions they had conducted during 1936–39. In fact, these early German operations had shown deficiencies almost as woeful as those demonstrated by Anglo-French forces in 1940 – but by the latter date the Germans had learned effectively from these failures.

The result was a Nazi military force that, while still far from perfect, was better honed than those of its opponents. The outcome of the 1940 campaign, while not inevitable, was predictable. Aided by an excellent strategic plan, the Germans achieved one of the most stunning triumphs in military history, achieving in six weeks the very goal – defeating France – that had eluded them during the entire Great War.

Now Britain was left to face Germany alone. The key weakness of the German war machine was, however, its lack of balance. German naval power remained weak in comparison with the Royal Navy and, despite its success in occupying Norway during April 1940, Germany had neither the amphibious assault capability nor the intimate inter-service coordination necessary to invade the United Kingdom. As an absolute prerequisite, the Luftwaffe had to neutralize RAF Fighter Command, but Hitler frittered away German air power during the Battle of Britain in retaliatory air strikes against British cities, rather than striking British airfields and coastal radar stations. Moreover, Hitler, who was (relatively speaking) an Anglophile who viewed his fellow "Anglo-Saxons" as racial cousins, never wholeheartedly committed himself to Operation Sea Lion, the invasion of Britain.

In late summer 1940, therefore, Hitler turned his attention to what had always been his ultimate goal: the titanic genocidal struggle to eliminate the Soviet Union and Communism, to enslave the Slavic peoples, and to acquire the "living space" (*Lebensraum*) crucial for the survival of the thousand-year Reich. Hitler expanded and honed his army into one of the best fighting forces that the world has ever seen and then, in his June 22, 1941, Barbarossa invasion, unleashed it against the Soviet Union. The German armored spearheads advanced to the gates of Leningrad and Moscow, while in the rear areas Axis forces enacted a brutal campaign of subjugation and ethnic cleansing: everywhere, this brutality drove the desperate Soviet peoples into the arms of the Communists.

Prior to launching their amphibious assault on the English coast, the Germans first needed to secure air superiority to protect their invasion barges from the Royal Navy. Luckily for Britain, the determined pilots of Fighter Command fought off the efforts initiated by Göring's Luftwaffe to defeat them. (Ann Ronan Picture Library)

The debacle of Stalingrad was the German army's worst setback of the war up to that point. It was also a personal disaster for those soldiers forced to surrender to the Soviets, since few of them survived Soviet captivity to return home during the mid-1950s. (AKG Berlin)

Unfortunately for the Germans, the Soviet Union could not be conquered in a single "Blitzkrieg" campaign, as Poland and France had been, due to both its size and the fierce resistance fostered by German viciousness. Overconfidence and ideologically driven racist arrogance that denigrated Soviet capabilities pervaded the German leadership, and this fueled the error of pursuing absolute and hence unachievable objectives. Thus, the Germans failed to pursue the effective political subversion that had directly contributed to their victory in the east during the Great War when in 1917 they dispatched Lenin to spread Bolshevism in Russia. In 1941 Stalin's unpopular regime remained as vulnerable to internal subversion as had the Tsar's, but ideologically driven German excesses against even anti-Russian Soviet minorities allowed Stalin and the Communists to rally all the various Soviet peoples behind them.

In his arrogance, Hitler had not prepared for the long, total war that was necessary to annihilate the Soviet Union; and nor did he totally mobilize until 1943–44, by which time it was too late. During 1942 the Soviets husbanded their strength as the Germans unwisely pushed deep into the Caucasus and to Stalingrad, greatly lengthening an already overextended front. In mid-November the Red Army struck back, routed the ill-equipped Romanian air forces north and south of Stalingrad, and encircled the Sixth Army in the city. German relief efforts failed as the Soviets attacked across the entire southern flank and drove back the Germans to the Mius River and to Kharkov. Here, German ripostes managed to stabilize the front again.

The war in the east reached its turning point during summer 1943 when Hitler threw away the first fruits of total war mobilization in an unwise and fully

Strategic situation in Europe, June 6, 1944

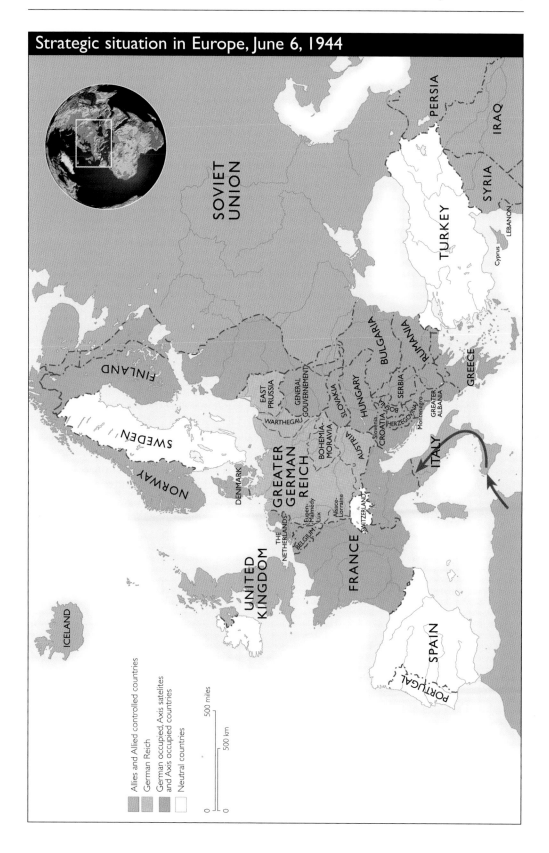

PERSIA

IRAQ

SYRIA

LEBANON

Cyprus

TURKEY

SOVIET UNION

FINLAND

SWEDEN

NORWAY

DENMARK

EAST PRUSSIA

GENERAL GOUVERNEMENT

WARTHEGAU

SLOVAKIA

BOHEMIA MORAVIA

GREATER GERMAN REICH

AUSTRIA

HUNGARY

BULGARIA

RUMANIA

SERBIA

BOSNIA HERZEGOVINA

Slovenia

CROATIA

Montenegro

GREATER ALBANIA

GREECE

ITALY

Eupen-Malmedy

Alsace-Lorraine

SWITZERLAND

THE NETHERLANDS

BELGIUM Lux.

FRANCE

UNITED KINGDOM

ICELAND

SPAIN

PORTUGAL

Allies and Allied controlled countries

German Reich

German occupied, Axis satelites and Axis occupied countries

Neutral countries

0   500 miles

0   500 km

anticipated counteroffensive at Kursk, which the Red Army stopped dead in its tracks. Thereafter, Soviet forces assumed the offensive all along the front and steadily drove the Germans back toward the prewar frontier. By spring 1944 the Germans were fully on the defensive with attenuated forces and could not now prevail in the east.

Meanwhile, a less brutal war was being waged in the Mediterranean. Hitler had little interest in this theater and was only drawn reluctantly into the region due to the military failures of his Axis partner, fascist Italy. A struggle of widely fluctuating fortunes materialized during 1941–42, but Hitler never committed the resources to overrun the British in North Africa, nor were Axis lines of communication secure enough to achieve this. Hitler's reluctance to commit forces to this southern flank ensured that the Axis failed to conquer Malta, which allowed the Allies to continue contesting the central and eastern Mediterranean.

With their lines of communication increasingly imperiled, the Axis powers were forced on the defensive in North Africa and then, during autumn 1942, were driven back toward the west. Finally, in November Allied forces landed in French Northwest Africa in Operation Torch and began to strangle into defeat the German forces then retiring into Tunisia. In May 1943, cut off from aerial and maritime resupply, the remaining Axis forces in Tunisia capitulated.

The Western Allies, still inexperienced, continued peripheral attacks aimed at wearing down the enemy. Allied amphibious attacks captured Sicily during July 1943 and then secured a beachhead on the Italian mainland during September. The Allies then slowly advanced up the peninsula of Italy until they bogged down at the strong German Winter Line defenses that ran from Naples through the Liri valley. The highly defensible terrain of Italy, the narrowness of the peninsula, and the rough parity in forces committed ensured that the Allies had no real prospect of rapid success in this theater.

The Mediterranean campaign did, however, divert German forces from the west, where since November 1943 the Germans had been desperately preparing to thwart an Allied invasion of France, which they knew would come during mid-1944. For the Western Allies, the decisive campaign of the war was about to begin. If the Germans could repulse the Allied invasion, then they could throw their armies in the west against the Red Army, hopefully halt the Soviet juggernaut, and perhaps still achieve an acceptable negotiated peace. The outcome of the war thus hinged on the Allied invasion of France.

A military audit

The Northwest Europe campaign pitted the armed forces of the Western Allies against the Wehrmacht, the Nazi German military. The combined Allied contingents were called the Allied Expeditionary Forces and comprised troops from the United States, the United Kingdom, Canada, France, Poland, the Netherlands, Belgium, and Czechoslovakia. The American General Dwight Eisenhower commanded the Supreme Headquarters, Allied Expeditionary Forces (SHAEF). General Bernard Montgomery served as the Land Forces Commander during the initial landings until September 1 when the position passed to Eisenhower.

Montgomery led the Anglo-Canadian 21st Army Group, which from July 1944 fielded three armies: the US First Army led by General Omar Bradley; the British Second Army under Miles "Bimbo" Dempsey; and the Canadian First Army under General Henry Crerar. On August 1, 1944, Bradley took command of the 12th US Army Group with the First Army (General Courtney Hodges)

The heads of state of the three main Allied contingents in northwest Europe: from left to right, Canadian Prime Minister W. L. Mackenzie King, American President Franklin Roosevelt, and British Prime Minister Winston Churchill. (Imperial War Museum H32129)

The Allied senior command team for the Northwest Europe campaign meet for the first time in London in January 1944. From left to right, the team included (top row) General Omar Bradley, Admiral Bertram Ramsay, Air Marshall Trafford Leigh-Mallory, General Walter Bedell-Smith, and (bottom row) Air Marshal Arthur Conningham, Supreme Commander Dwight Eisenhower, and General Bernard Montgomery. (ISI)

and Third Army (General George Patton) under command. When, during September, the forces pushing northeast from the French Mediterranean coast linked up with those advancing east from Normandy, the 6th US Army Group, led by General Jacob Devers, and comprising the American Seventh Army and French First Army, came under Eisenhower's control. Later still, the American Ninth and Fifteenth Armies joined Bradley's army group.

Admiral Sir Bertram Ramsay controlled the vast invasion armada and naval covering forces. Air Chief Marshal Sir Trafford Leigh-Mallory commanded the Allied Expeditionary Air Forces, comprising the Royal Air Force, the US Army Air Force, and the Royal Canadian Air Force. Tactical

aviation belonging to the US IX and XIX Tactical Air Commands and the Anglo-Canadian Second Tactical Air Force supported the ground battle. The heavy bombers of RAF Bomber Command and the Eighth United States Army Air Force provided additional assistance.

The German Commander-in-Chief West, Field Marshal Gerd von Rundstedt, exercised nominal control over the Wehrmacht in France, Belgium, and Holland. His ground

As Commander-in-Chief West, Field Marshal Gerd von Rundstedt exercised nominal authority over all of the German armed forces in western Europe. In reality, however, his three subordinate ground commanders – including Army Group B commander Erwin Rommel – as well as his theater air force and naval commanders all enjoyed considerable freedom of action. (AKG Berlin)

German dispositions in the west, June 6, 1944

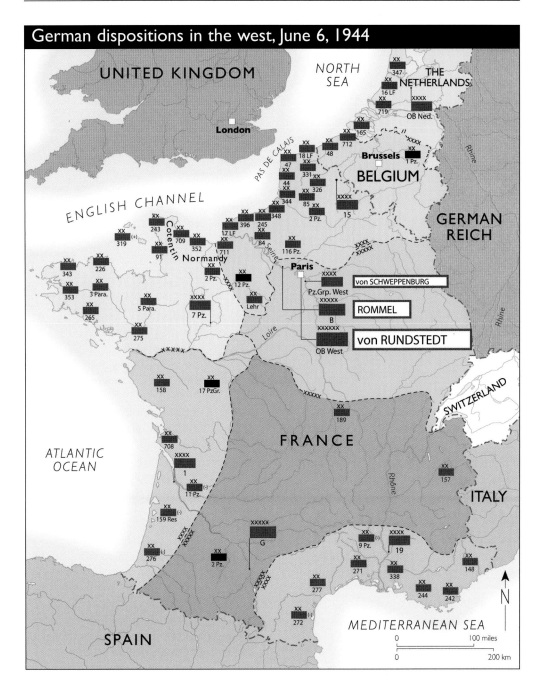

forces belonged to three separate commands. Field Marshal Erwin Rommel's Army Group B comprised the Seventh Army in Brittany and Normandy and the Fifteenth Army deployed from Le Havre along the Pas de Calais to the Scheldt. The independent LXXXVIII Corps defended the Netherlands. Finally came Army Group G, comprising the First Army deployed along the western Atlantic coast and the Nineteenth Army defending the southern French Mediterranean coast.

In addition, General Geyr von Schweppenburg's Panzer Group West controlled the mechanized reserves who were tasked with driving the invaders back into the sea. Further complicating the

Field Marshal Erwin Rommel – the "Desert Fox" – commanded Army Group B in northern France and Belgium. He was not impressed with large sections of the Atlantic Wall defenses, and in the months prior to the D-Day landings he channeled his iron determination into strengthening these coastal defenses. (AKG Berlin)

ground organization was the fact that four of the 10 mechanized divisions in the west were designated as Armed Forces High Command (OKW) reserves, and it required Hitler's permission before these could be committed to combat.

Admiral Kranke's Naval High Command West orchestrated the Kriegsmarine's counterinvasion measures. German Navy assets in western Europe comprised numerous small surface vessels, 40 U-boats, and many naval coast artillery batteries. German aircraft in the west belonged to General Sperrle's III Air Fleet. Decimated by sustained aerial combat during 1943–44 while opposing the Allied bomber offensive against the Reich, the Luftwaffe had only a few hundred planes available to defend French airspace.

The Allies had a significant numerical superiority in troops, heavy weapons, logistics, air power, and naval assets. The Kriegsmarine and Luftwaffe might be able to achieve local successes, but they were so heavily outnumbered that they were unable to contest the invasion. Mastery of the skies allowed the Allies to launch an increasingly effective strategic bombing campaign against the German war economy and transportation network. Such attacks had already essentially isolated the Normandy invasion area prior to D-Day, and the dwindling German ability to bring up fresh troops and supplies to the fighting front became an increasingly debilitating weakness as the campaign progressed.

The Germans, on the other hand, would rarely molest the Allied war economy in the last 18 months of the war. Moreover, as a result of the code-breaking successes of "Ultra," the Allies had excellent intelligence about German dispositions and intentions, while the Germans possessed a woefully inadequate intelligence picture.

Despite these significant advantages, however, Allied victory was not a foregone conclusion. The Germans enjoyed a qualitative edge, at least in ground forces, early in the campaign – although this edge was blunted during the campaign. The Allied armies in June 1944 had yet to reach peak effectiveness, and so could not yet engage the *Westheer* on equal terms.

Montgomery presided over a flawed British army whose development had been stunted between the wars and had been unable to cope with German offensives. It had therefore suffered serious defeats early in the war in Norway, France, North Africa, Malaysia, and Burma. Only with difficulty had the army recovered from these setbacks and fully learned the lessons of modern war during 1942–44. Consequently, Montgomery was acutely aware that his army's morale remained vulnerable. The army had also only been on the sustained offensive for a little over a year and was still developing proficiency in the complex art of attacking stout German defenses.

Additionally, Montgomery was cognizant of the finite nature of British resources. The nation had already been at war for nearly five years and was conducting simultaneous military operations in multiple theaters across the globe. Montgomery was determined to avoid the catastrophic casualties suffered during the World War I, from which Britain had neither psychologically nor materially fully recovered.

British military operations were therefore dominated by personnel concerns as its manpower dried up. Montgomery clearly understood that all available reserves would be consumed during the campaign and that his command would become a wasting asset. The manpower situation was even more acute for the Canadians, and of course very few replacements were available for the continental contingents fighting alongside the Allies, as they were all forces in exile.

These constraints powerfully shaped Montgomery's conduct of the campaign. He devised a cautious theater strategy where the Allies would use their numerical and material superiority to wear down the enemy in a protracted attritional battle. Montgomery eschewed a bold maneuver warfare strategy that might have won the war more quickly but ran the risk of increasing casualties. The result was a careful and controlled approach to operations that enabled the Germans to organize effective defensive positions as they withdrew.

The American military, on the other hand, had far greater resources. After their setback at the Kasserine Pass in January 1943, the Americans had steadily gained the upper hand over the Germans. Eisenhower's forces therefore had more confidence and better morale. The American military tradition had long emphasized direct offensive action. In fact its aggressive, offensive doctrine ensured that American troops sometimes lacked the respect for the enemy that the British had learned through painful experience. The biggest problem the Americans faced was their inexperience. Only a tiny fraction of the forces earmarked for the Normandy campaign had previously seen action.

Another deficiency was doctrinal. Interwar technological changes – particularly the development of mechanized forces and air power – fundamentally challenged military doctrine in the American army. Despite its endeavors, when it entered the World War II, the army had not yet worked out how to integrate armor and air power fully in support of ground operations. Combat in the Mediterranean quickly exposed these flaws in doctrine; yet, effective solutions to these problems were still emerging during summer 1944.

The audit of war also illuminated the inefficiency of the American manpower replacement system, which was unable to restore rapidly fighting power to depleted formations. The problem of sustaining combat power was aggravated by the American government's shortsighted decision to limit the wartime army to just 90 divisions, a policy that forced formations to stay in the front line indefinitely, rather than being rotated out for rest and replenishment. A combination of inexperience, doctrinal deficiencies, and a poor manpower replacement system ensured that the US army in June 1944 was not yet able to bring its full fighting power to bear.

Given its greater resources and aggressive, offensive doctrine, the American military naturally assumed the larger role in the campaign, increasingly so as it progressed. It was to spearhead the Allied breakout once a permanent lodgment had been achieved. All the armies of the Western Allies learned through trial and error to fight more proficiently as the northwest Europe campaign progressed, thereby narrowing and ultimately eradicating the German qualitative edge. It was the US army, however, that proved able to adapt and enhance its combat effectiveness most rapidly. By the latter stages of the Northwest Europe campaign, it was able to outfight rather than simply overwhelm an increasingly outnumbered and outgunned enemy. This ability to adapt and enhance its combat effectiveness ensured that the USA emerged preeminent within the coalition by 1945.

Defeating the Nazi military force, however, was never going to be easy or quick. The German defenders had the benefit of considerable combat experience, and a realistic, proven doctrine and tactics refined through years of war. Operating under a totalitarian regime, the military potentially had all the resources of the state at its disposal. Moreover, the Germans were a martial people with a long and proud military history. Nevertheless, the Nazi war machine was by no means invincible; nor were its soldiers the "supermen" that racist Nazi propaganda extolled them to be.

In reality, the German military fought in northwest Europe under severe constraints. Brutal attrition in the east had already torn the heart out of the Wehrmacht and it was scraping the manpower and resources barrels by 1944. But its biggest deficiencies were logistical. Constant combat ensured that the Germans lacked the supplies necessary for victory and throughout the campaign they

operated on a logistical shoestring, particularly liquid fuels. Moreover, the German war economy had long been inefficient and poorly managed. While dramatic increases in production had recently been realized by ruthless rationalization, the German war economy was now subject to punishing Allied heavy bomber attacks and was unable to meet the needs of a three-front war. Consequently, the German military remained perennially short of the means of conducting modern operations. It was rarely able to contest Allied aerial supremacy, which hindered all German ground operations and denied them information about the enemy.

German commanders, therefore, remained woefully ignorant of enemy actions and intentions, which hampered German countermeasures. Attrition had also badly denuded German ground forces of vehicles, reducing the strategic mobility that had hitherto allowed German forces to evade annihilation by a numerically superior enemy. This dwindling mobility progressively increased the vulnerability of German formations to encirclement and annihilation by a far more mobile enemy.

These deficiencies ensured that the German military was unable to mount the combined-arms defense necessary to prevail in the west, and that instead it would slowly be driven back in grim attritional warfare. Nonetheless, the determination of German troops and commanders, their professionalism, as well as their realistic doctrine, tactics, and training allowed them to offer sustained, stubborn resistance that cost the Allies dearly. Influenced by Nazi racism and propaganda, as well as the instinct for self-preservation, German troops continued to fight to protect their families at home from the vengeance that they feared the Allies would exact for the horrible measures the Nazis had taken to keep Europe under control. The Germans could be expected to fight long and hard. And even if they could not win, they could at least postpone the inevitable for as long as possible and increase the price of the enemy's victory.

The Allies invade France

The Allied armed forces required extensive preparation before they could successfully invade Nazi-occupied France. During 1940–41 the British military was fully preoccupied preparing to thwart an anticipated German invasion of Britain. Only when that threat receded, after Hitler's June 1941 invasion of the Soviet Union, could the British armed forces contemplate a return to the continent.

However, other struggles continued to preoccupy British forces. At sea, the Battle of the Atlantic raged, threatening Britain's maritime communications, until the Allies exorcised the U-boat threat during 1943. In the skies, the Allies had to contend with continued periodic German air raids across the Channel. Moreover, Britain found itself

Britain had to secure strategic success over the German U-boat menace as well as the German Navy's commerce raiding surface fleet before serious preparations could begin for any future amphibious landing on the coast of Nazi-occupied Europe. (AKG Berlin)

engaged in ongoing ground combat in both Burma and North Africa – operations that diverted troops and resources away from Britain. It was therefore not until 1943 that invasion preparations hit high gear.

Even then much work needed to be done. The British army commanders had to inculcate the troops with the important lessons of modern war that had been so painfully relearned in North Africa. The army had to reequip with new weaponry; formations had to reorganize to enhance their fighting power; and for the first time, troops undertook offensive training geared toward continental warfare.

British air, ground, and naval forces also had to learn to work smoothly together to establish the effective interservice cooperation that was essential for victory. But building good teamwork required long association to develop full understanding of the respective capabilities and limitations of

each service. Each branch of the army – infantry, artillery, and armor – had not only to improve its doctrine and training, but also to put aside regimental tribalism to work together effectively.

The D-Day amphibious assault also required extensive preparation. Initially, the Allies greatly underestimated the difficulties this entailed. They were rudely disabused of such complacency during the August 1942 Dieppe raid, in which the 2nd Canadian Division was badly mauled attacking a well-defended German-held port. The most important lesson of Dieppe was that a heavily defended harbor was too tough a nut to crack. The Allies therefore decided to land adjacent to a major port and establish a firm lodgment, before seizing the harbor that would be vital to the long-term logistical sustainability of the bridgehead. After considerable debate, the Allies chose Normandy, with its major port of Cherbourg, as the invasion site.

The Dieppe raid also demonstrated the need for specialized amphibious assault armor to crack the enemy's beach defenses; for, at Dieppe, the supporting tanks proved unable to get off the beach to assist the troops as they advanced inland. Over the next year Britain devoted considerable resources to developing these vehicles. Dieppe equally revealed the need for fire support during the actual landing. In the lead-up to D-Day, the Allied navies developed and refined elaborate procedures to deliver naval gunfire during the landings. They built special landing craft, equipped with guns and rockets to augment naval gunfire. Assembling, organizing, and preparing an amphibious armada of thousands of vessels took many months to complete.

The Royal Air Force (RAF) also had an important role to play. Having won the Battle of Britain in 1940, Fighter Command needed a new mission and found it in the direct, tactical support of ground forces on the battlefield. Such support had proven woefully deficient in the early desert battles, to such an extent that British troops derided the RAF as the "Royal Absent Force."

Initially, technical problems – including the unsuitability of aircraft, lack of air–ground coordination, and poor aerial recognition skills – seriously hampered the utility of tactical aviation. Only through a difficult process of trial and error were solutions to these problems found. By D-Day, however, Allied air power was ready to provide extensive and sustained tactical air support.

The RAF leadership, however, remained loath to divert Bomber Command from its nocturnal area bombing of Germany's cities, which was intended to break civilian morale. This reflected the powerful sway of interwar strategic bombing theorists, who held that the heavy bomber "would always get through" to its target and that, consequently, strategic bombing was capable of winning

Air Marshal Harris, head of Bomber Command, spearheaded Britain's strategic bombing offensive against Germany, which was designed to break the morale of Germany's civilian population. During the Northwest Europe campaign, Bomber Command also employed its heavy bombers in direct support of Montgomery's offensives, most notably during Operation Goodwood in July 1944. (AKG Berlin)

wars unaided. The result of this dogma was increasingly heavy night attacks by the RAF and daylight precision raids by the US Army Air Force against German industrial centers.

The Germans, however, were unwilling to accept that the bomber would always get through. During 1943 they developed a potent air defense system that involved

Allied aerial interdiction attacks were so successful in the weeks prior to D-Day that virtually every bridge over the Loire and Seine rivers into Normandy had been put out of action. This accomplishment severely dislocated Rommel's ability to get reinforcements to the invasion front line. Of course, when the Allies came to cross the Seine in August 1944, they had to construct new pontoon bridges like the one depicted here in the foreground. (Imperial War Museum B9748)

specialized night fighters vectored onto bomber streams by ground-based early warning radar. The result over winter 1943–44 was the infliction of loss rates that Bomber Command could not sustain indefinitely. American daylight raids also began to suffer correspondingly heavy losses. The solution was long-range fighter protection, but it was not until the development of the P-51 Mustang external fuel tanks that it proved possible for fighters to stay with the bombers all the way to their German targets.

The attrition that Allied heavy bombers suffered over winter 1943–44 had two unanticipated benefits, however. The first was the destruction of the German fighter

force in western Europe by Allied long-range fighter escorts as the enemy planes came up to engage the bombers. Victory in this attritional struggle gave the Allies the aerial supremacy they needed to guarantee success in the invasion. Second, the heavy attrition softened Bomber Command's dogmatic opposition to employing strategic air power in support of the Normandy invasion. Thus, during spring 1944 heavy bombers joined tactical aviation – fighters, fighter-bombers, and medium bombers – in a massive aerial interdiction campaign intended to isolate the Normandy battlefield. By D-Day, despite consciously dissipating their strikes to disguise the location of the invasion, Allied air attacks had destroyed virtually every rail bridge over the Loire and Seine rivers into Normandy, thus severely hampering the German ability to move forces to repel the invasion.

The task that the American military faced was even greater, for in 1943 the US army had very few combat-ready troops in Britain and these lacked the support services necessary for offensive amphibious operations. The USA had only entered the war in December 1941 and sustained peacetime neglect had ensured that its armed services required considerable time to shape up for overseas deployment. Moreover, no sooner had American forces arrived in Britain in 1942 than they were immediately committed to combat in the Mediterranean during Operation Torch, the November 1942 invasion of French northwest Africa. After eventual victory in Tunisia during May 1943, in what proved a difficult baptism of fire for inexperienced American forces, US troops helped capture Sicily during July–August 1943 and then invaded Italy that September.

It was therefore not until the autumn of 1943 that veteran formations could be withdrawn from the Mediterranean to prepare for Operation Overlord, as the Normandy invasion had now been designated. In the meantime, a massive buildup of American forces in Britain occurred, including the enormous quantities of ordnance, ammunition, fuel, rations, and

spare parts needed to sustain operations. American forces gathered in western England adjacent to their ports of arrival, and logistic considerations more than anything else determined that American forces would land on the right (western) flank of the invasion.

American troops also worked hard in the year before D-Day to overcome the flaws in their combat performance demonstrated in the Mediterranean. The biggest weakness in that theater had been the inadequate tactical air support caused by the lack of air–ground communication, poor aerial recognition skills, and inexperience. Combat revealed doctrinal problems within the army relating to new technology, particularly tanks and tank destroyers, and identified serious shortcomings in the American replacement system. During 1943–44, the American military worked strenuously to rectify these deficiencies.

For the German defenders, extensive preparations to thwart the invasion began even later. During 1943 the German High Command continued to believe that the Allies were neither materially nor psychologically ready to launch the Second Front. The Germans therefore only modestly enhanced their Atlantic Wall defenses, the allegedly formidable fortifications along the Atlantic coast. Unfortunately for the Germans, the Atlantic Wall existed only adjacent to the major ports; otherwise it remained largely a fiction of Nazi propaganda.

Instead, the German Army in the West – the *Westheer* – remained a backwater of the Nazi war effort. Its primary mission remained supporting the ongoing (and increasingly disastrous) war on the Eastern Front. Throughout 1943 the Germans continued to use France to rehabilitate formations shattered in the east and to work up new divisions to operational readiness, prior to deployment to the Soviet Union and, from September 1943, also to Italy.

The permanent German occupation forces in France thus comprised second-rate coastal defense divisions of limited manpower, firepower, and mobility. Almost no significant operational reserve existed in the west, besides refitting or newly forming mechanized formations. German naval power likewise consisted primarily of numerous small coastal vessels that were incapable of turning back a major invasion force. Moreover, the few German aircraft deployed in the west remained fully preoccupied trying to thwart the Allied air onslaught on the cities and economic infrastructure of Germany. Thus the German military in 1943 was incapable of stopping the Allies if they invaded. Yet, this unsatisfactory position reflected German awareness that the Allies were not yet ready to invade, even if they had wanted to.

This situation changed during November 1943 when Hitler recognized the inevitability of an Allied invasion attempt during 1944 and switched Germany's strategic priority to the west. Over the next seven months there materialized a massive influx of veterans and new recruits as well as Germany's latest and most lethal weapons. The result would be a metamorphosis of German combat power in the west.

By June 1944 the Germans had built up sufficient strength potentially to thwart an invasion: if, that is, they gained some advance warning of where and when the enemy was going to strike, so that they could launch a concentrated counteroffensive to throw the Allies back into the sea. Yet success also required that the German air force and navy at least disrupt Allied mastery of the seas and the skies. The gravest German weakness, however, remained its woefully inadequate logistical base, which, exacerbated by the Allied aerial interdiction campaign, ensured that the Germans lacked the supply stockpiles to win a protracted battle of attrition.

From D-Day to victory

On D-Day, June 6, 1944, six Allied infantry divisions, heavily reinforced with artillery and armor, and supported by a massive air umbrella and naval gunfire, landed astride five invasion beaches. American troops assaulted "Utah" beach on the southern tip of the Cotentin peninsula and at "Omaha" along the western Calvados coast. Anglo-Canadian troops landed on "Gold," "Juno," and "Sword" beaches between Arromanches and Ouistreham in front of Caen. In addition, the Allies dropped one British and two American airborne divisions along both flanks of the invasion to disrupt German counterattacks aimed at rolling up the beachheads.

The Allied forces experienced contrasting fates on D-Day. Anglo-Canadian forces firmly established themselves ashore on their three assault beaches, but failed to achieve the ambitious goal of capturing the key city of Caen. Although the invaders breached the bulk of the defenses, the Germans held the Pèriers Ridge and prevented the linking up of the "Gold" and "Sword" beachheads. Along the ridge that afternoon elements of the 21st Panzer Division counterattacked and successfully pushed through to the coast. But outnumbered and with both flanks unsecured, the Germans retired to the ridge after dark. Moreover, the landing of the British 6th Airborne Division east of the Orne protected the vulnerable left flank of the landing against a weak armored counterattack that the Germans launched that day.

For American forces, the invasion did not go quite as smoothly. At "Utah" beach, Americans troops quickly established a solid beachhead; however, at "Omaha" beach, the landing came close to being repulsed. The difficult terrain of steep bluffs bisected by narrow ravines, the loss of most of the amphibious assault armor in rough seas, and the failure of the aerial bombing attacks left the initial assault waves pinned down by murderous German defensive fire. Ultimately, sheer numbers, toughness and heroism, backed by short-range naval gunfire, overwhelmed the defenders and allowed American forces to establish a shallow enclave ashore.

Reflecting the inherent hazard of airborne operations, the drop of the American 82nd and 101st Airborne Divisions inland behind "Utah" beach and astride the Merderet River became highly scattered and casualties were heavy. The dispersion did have one inadvertent benefit, however, for it confused the Germans as to the real location of the invasion. Though widely scattered, the paratroopers dislocated German communications and prevented a major counterattack against "Utah" beach on D-Day, allowing the landing troops to establish a firm foothold ashore.

Other factors contributed to Allied success. The absence of many senior German commanders at a war game in Brittany and the disruption of communications due to aerial and naval bombardment both hampered German countermeasures. As significantly, Allied domination of the skies prevented the Luftwaffe from effectively impeding the invasion. The German navy proved equally unable to resist the vast invasion armada. In sum, months of meticulous preparation combined with personal heroism, massive air and naval support, and the achievement of surprise, brought success on D-Day. By the end of June 6, 1944, though few recognized it at the time, the Allies had established a permanent foothold in France.

D-Day, June 6, 1944

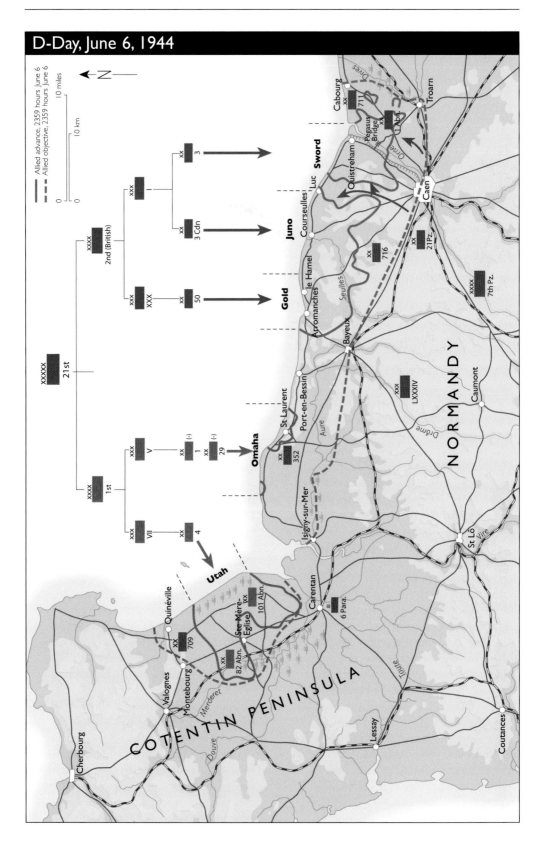

The aftermath of D-Day

After D-Day, little went according to plan. Montgomery's advance quickly stalled when powerful German armored reserves converged on Caen to smash the Anglo-Canadian beachhead. While his forces repulsed these counterattacks, his forces could not gain ground and the struggle for Caen degenerated into a grim six-week attritional battle. Hitler and his commanders believed that the outcome of the campaign hinged on holding Caen, so the Germans massed their best formations opposite the British sector. The narrow bridgehead gave the Germans a relatively short front, allowing them to develop defenses in depth that presented Montgomery with a considerable challenge. Meanwhile, they rushed the II SS Panzer Corps from the

Operation Goodwood remains one of the most controversial offensives of the Normandy campaign. Although the abortive British attack to secure Caen and the Bourguébus Ridge suffered very high tank losses, it did facilitate the success of the subsequent American Cobra offensive in the west of the Normandy theater. (NARA)

Eastern Front for a counteroffensive to smash the bridgehead. In the interim, the Germans stubbornly defended Caen to deny Anglo-Canadian forces room to maneuver.

Neither did American operations go according to plan after D-Day. The Germans temporarily checked the advance of General "Lightning" Joe Collins' VII Corps from "Utah" beach toward the key port of Cherbourg along the Quineville Ridge. The advance of Major-General Leonard Gerow's V US Corps on St. Lô from "Omaha" beach was likewise slow. After Isigny fell on June 9, the way to St. Lô stood open, but American caution allowed German reserves to move up and build a new defensive front. Moreover, the priority accorded to Collins' advance on Cherbourg hindered the drive on St. Lô. Consequently, the V Corps offensive abruptly ground to a halt 2 miles (3.2 km) short of St. Lô on June 18.

The slow advance on Cherbourg forced Collins to abandon the planned direct advance on the port. Instead, on June 15, VII Corps struck west and cut the peninsula two days later, isolating Cherbourg. Only then, on June 22, did Collins launch an

all-out three-division attack on the port. Though the attenuated defenders fought fiercely, final resistance ceased on July 1. Although the Americans had finally captured their much-needed major harbor, they had done so well behind schedule and the enemy had left the port in ruins.

On June 26, along the eastern flank, Montgomery launched his first major offensive, Operation Epsom. It was an ambitious attack to breach the strong enemy defenses west of Caen, force the Orne and Odon rivers, gain the high ground southwest of the city and thereby outflank it. The VIII Corps of Lieutenant-General Miles Dempsey's Second (British) Army spearheaded the offensive backed by strong air, naval, and artillery support. Yet bad luck dogged Epsom: unseasonably bad weather forced Montgomery to attack without the planned air bombardment and the neighboring XXX Corps failed to take the

flanking Rauray Ridge, which hindered the entire attack.

Significant concentration of force finally allowed the British infantry to penetrate the thin German defenses and establish a bridgehead across the Odon River. Thereafter, the 11th Armored Division pushed through and captured Hill 112 beyond. By June 28, Montgomery had torn a 5-mile (8 km) gap in the German defenses. But the methodical advance prevented Montgomery from achieving further gains.

Next, after German reserves had counterattacked the narrow British corridor and the shallow Odon bridgehead, the cautious Montgomery abandoned Hill 112

In order to avoid high casualties, Montgomery favored the use of massive aerial and artillery firepower to support his ground offensives. The effect on urban centers such as Caen, shown here, was devastating. (Imperial War Museum, B7754)

and retired to a shorter, more defensible line. Subsequently, between June 29 and July 2, VIII Corps repulsed strong, if poorly coordinated, German attacks that constituted the long-anticipated enemy counteroffensive. The newly arrived II SS Panzer Corps hurled itself against the British Odon bridgehead, but made little headway in the face of tremendous Allied defensive artillery fire, and the operation soon fizzled out.

The German counterattack failed primarily because the Germans only had supplies for a few days of sustained offensive action and because they had attacked prematurely with new troops unfamiliar with Normandy's combat conditions. The counteroffensive's failure proved unequivocally that the Allied lodgment had become permanent. Therefore, Hitler devised a new strategy: an unyielding defense to corral the Allies into a narrow bridgehead

and deny them the room and favorable terrain for mobile operations. This decision committed the Germans to an attritional battle within range of the Allied fleet; it was a battle they could not win.

However, Montgomery had neither broken through nor gained the high ground over the Odon in Epsom. It was not until July 8 that he launched a new multi-corps attack on Caen, designated Charnwood. Montgomery again relied heavily on air power to shatter enemy resistance. A strategic bomber raid destroyed several Orne bridges and sharply reduced the Germans'

The Allies' employment of massive aerial and artillery firepower inflicted considerable damage on the defending Germans. However, the extensive cratering such tactics caused also hampered Allied attempts to advance deep through the enemy's defensive position. (Imperial War Museum CL 838)

ability to resupply their forces in the northern part of the city. Meanwhile, Anglo-Canadian forces launched concentric attacks on the beleaguered and greatly outnumbered defenders. Inexorably, superior numbers and firepower drove the enemy back, and on July 9 Montgomery's troops finally fought their way into northern Caen, four weeks behind schedule. However, Montgomery's exhausted forces were unable to push across the defensible Orne River barrier onto the open Falaise Plain beyond.

Despite reinforcement by Collins' VII Corps, and fresh divisions from Britain, General Omar Bradley's First US Army still struggled to advance in the *bocage* hedgerows when it renewed its offensive toward St. Lô on July 3. Major-General Troy Middleton's fresh VIII US Corps struck south from the base of the Cotentin peninsula with three divisions and in five days took La Haye-du-Puits against stiff resistance. But ferocious opposition stopped the offensive at the Ay and Seves rivers on July 15 . Simultaneously, VII Corps attacked from Carentan toward Pèriers on July 3, but quickly stalled due to poor weather and difficult marshy terrain. Even after the veteran 4th Division joined the attack on July 5, VII Corps gained only 750 yards (700 m) in four days. The Germans both defended skillfully and counterattacked repeatedly to sap American strength. Though it beat off these counterattacks during July 10–12, VII Corps had to go over to defense on July 15.

Gradually, however, American forces solved the problems of hedgerow fighting with improved tactics, enhanced firepower, and better coordination, all of which speeded the fall of St. Lô. Major-General Charles Corlett's newly arrived XIX US Corps struck south with three divisions on July 7 to capture St. Jean-de-Daye. Thereafter, the corps slowly, but inexorably, gained ground until it cut the Pèriers–St. Lô highway on July 20. The 29th US Division, after renewing its drive toward St. Lô on July 11, both seized the ridge that dominated the northeastern approaches to the city, and advanced across the St. Lô–Bayeux highway. On July 18, the hard-pressed Germans abandoned the city.

American forces had grimly fought their way forward into more open ground and were therefore in a position to prepare a major breakthrough operation, code-named Cobra.

While the Americans prepared for Cobra, Montgomery launched a major new offensive, named Goodwood, around Caen. This would become the campaign's most controversial operation. In this attack, Montgomery sought to capture both southern Caen and the Bourguébus Ridge – objectives that opened the way to the Falaise Plain to their south. A new attack was necessary to hold German reserves at Caen while the Americans prepared for their breakout bid. However, Montgomery required massive fire support to breach the strong German defenses behind the Orne and it was thus only on July 18 that he attacked out of the bridgehead east of the Orne, which his airborne troops had captured on D-Day. Unfortunately, this bridgehead was so constricted that it proved impossible to preserve surprise and therefore Montgomery had to rely heavily on air bombardment.

Goodwood was both ill-conceived and ill-executed. Aerial bombing and artillery fire enabled British armor to crash through the forward German defenses to the foot of the high ground south of Caen. But the outnumbered Germans nevertheless conducted a delaying withdrawal that disrupted and dispersed the British advance. Thus, British armor reached the Bourguébus Ridge late on July 18 with little infantry and no artillery support. The German gun line of heavy antitank and antiaircraft guns emplaced on the high ground then repulsed the British tanks, inflicting heavy losses. As dusk approached, German combined-arms counterattacks drove the British armor back with further heavy loss.

Montgomery attacked for two more days, but the advance had lost its momentum. Nowhere had his forces established a solid foothold on the vital Bourguébus Ridge, and the heavy losses suffered eroded British fighting power. In fact, the employment of massed armor against intact defenses brought catastrophic tank losses during Goodwood: more than one-third of British

The Normandy campaign, June 6–August 20, 1944

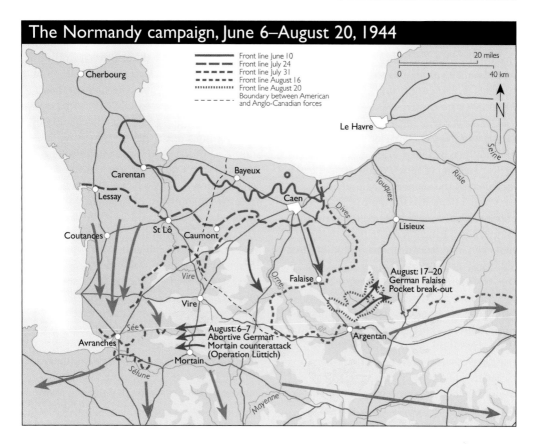

Front line June 10
Front line July 24
Front line July 31
Front line August 16
Front line August 20
Boundary between American and Anglo-Canadian forces

tank strength in Normandy. Moreover, the offensive failed to "write down" enemy armor as Montgomery had intended. Though Goodwood did gain more ground and temporarily pinned some German reserves on the Caen front, these limited achievements were bought at a price that British forces could not afford to repeat.

The Cobra breakout

Goodwood nevertheless helped the American breakout bid by diverting badly needed supplies from the St. Lô sector to the Caen front to replenish German forces after their heavy expenditures resisting Montgomery's attack. The result was serious erosion of the German logistic position on the American front prior to Cobra, which facilitated the American breakout. Allied air attacks had continually hampered German resupply operations, thus creating serious logistic

problems. This situation worsened, particularly on the western sector, after July 15 with the renewed destruction of the rail bridge at Tours, the German Seventh Army's major supply artery. Its supplies thus dwindled on the St. Lô front in the lead-up to Cobra. In fact, the defending German LXXXIV Corps had less than two days' fuel left. Thus for the first time in the campaign, during Cobra supply shortages crippled the German defenses and prevented them from cordoning off the American break-in during July 25–26, as they had all previous Allied offensives.

Innovation also aided the American success in Cobra. To provide the firepower it lacked, the First US Army relied first on carpet bombing to smash a hole in the German front; second, on a narrow front offensive to penetrate the German line; and lastly, on mobility and speed to outmaneuver, rather than outfight, the enemy. Bradley, thus, planned Cobra as a concentrated break-in attack by three infantry divisions on a narrow front, supported by intense air and artillery attack, to secure the flanks; meanwhile, three mechanized divisions would punch through to the rear, capture Coutances, and cut off the German LXXXIV Corps on the coast.

The preparatory carpet-bombing was the largest and most effective air attack on ground forces yet seen in the war. While faulty planning, sloppy execution, and bad luck dogged the aerial bombardment, it nevertheless crippled German communications and battered the forward-concentrated Panzer *Lehr* Division so much that even its seasoned troops could not resist VII Corps' concentrated attack. Consequently, the Americans advanced 2 miles (3.2 km) into the German defenses on July 25 and, subsequently, American speed and mobility turned this break-in into a breakout. During this exploitation phase, American forces reinforced their success faster than the Germans could redeploy reserves, as mounting logistic deficiencies for the first time crippled the enemy's defense. On July 26, VII Corps gained 5 miles (8 km) as the stretched German front began to collapse.

In response, the Germans rushed the XLVII Panzer Corps (2nd and 116th Panzer Divisions) from the British front to take the American breakthrough in the flank and nip off the penetration. But the American XIX Corps' flanking push south from St. Lô disrupted the planned German counterattack and forced the Germans to strike hastily amid the thick *bocage* southeast of St. Lô. Both the difficult terrain and mounting supply shortages frustrated the German counterattack, as the panzer forces experienced the same offensive difficulties that had earlier bedeviled American operations. The XLVII Panzer Corps proved unable to hold the ground taken: all it achieved was to build a defensive front facing west and await promised reinforcements.

On July 27 the Americans achieved a decisive breakthrough. As the enemy evacuated Lessay and Pèriers to rebuild a cohesive defense, VII US Corps advanced

12 miles (19 km) until it halted just short of Coutances. The next day, the corps captured Coutances and linked up with VII Corps. SS Colonel-General Paul Hausser, the German Seventh Army commander, then erred when he ordered LXXXIV Corps to fight its way southeast in an effort to regain a continuous front, instead of retiring unopposed due south to re-establish a new line south of Coutances. The retiring German forces thus ran into the American spearheads southeast of Coutances and were isolated in the Roncey pocket. With the German front torn open, Bradley expanded Cobra on July 29. VII and VIII Corps renewed their drive to the south and the next day crossed the Sienne River, took Avranches, and seized a bridgehead across the Sée River, before crossing the Sélune River at Pontaubault on July 31 to open the gateway to Brittany.

Montgomery also resumed the offensive in late July, hastily launching Operation Bluecoat, against the weakly held German front astride Caumont. This rapidly devised attack was intended to maintain pressure on the Germans and prevent the transfer of enemy armor against the Americans. Six divisions of VIII and XXX British Corps assaulted a single German infantry division, but the premature start meant that the attack lacked the massive artillery support that habitually accompanied British offensives. Moreover, though the German defense was weak, the front had been static since mid-June and the Germans had entrenched in depth amid the thick *bocage*.

Initially, British forces quickly penetrated the enemy lines and drew into battle German armor transferring to the American front. Yet, failure to take the flanking high ground at Amaye seriously hampered progress. Caution also prevented British forces from tearing open a barely coherent German front that was ripe to be shattered. On July 30, the British captured a bridgehead over the Souleuvre River on the undefended boundary between Seventh Army and Panzer Group West. For the next week the two German commands remained detached along this boundary, leaving a 2-mile (3.2 km) gap that the British failed to exploit. By the time the British had realized the weakness of the enemy and advanced, German reserves had closed the gap.

The position of the Allied boundary line also hindered a rapid British capture of Vire, imposing a delay that aided the enemy's retreat. The town's quick fall would have severed the enemy's lateral communications lines and seriously hampered the German withdrawal. While the 11th Armored Division of VIII Corps advanced steadily, XXX Corps' armor soon lagged behind, leaving the 11th Armored dangerously exposed as German resistance stiffened on August 1 with the arrival of armor from Caen. On August 6, German counterblows almost overran the 11th Armored Division's spearhead, but the German armor was keen to push on westward against the Americans and thus launched only limited counterattacks.

American reinforcements move up to Mortain to block the German "Lüttich" counterattack on August 7. This operation was one of Hitler's greatest strategic blunders. Unlikely ever to succeed, the operation merely sucked German forces farther west into the noose of an encirclement then forming in the Argentan–Falaise area; this ensured that the *Westheer* would suffer a catastrophic strategic defeat in Normandy during August 1944. (US Army)

On August 1, meanwhile, Bradley's 12th US Army Group became operational and assumed command of the First Army and General George Patton's new Third Army. American forces were now able to conduct the fast-paced mobile war for which the peacetime army had trained. While the First Army advanced southeast and occupied Mortain on August 3, Patton conducted a spectacular armored advance that first isolated Brittany and then pushed deep into the peninsula to seize Pontivy. Nonetheless, most of the enemy garrison was still able to retire into the ports of Brest, St. Malo, and Lorient.

Germany strikes back!

During the breakout, American forces for the first time assumed the defense to thwart a major German counteroffensive that aimed to seal off the American penetration and isolate Patton's command. The American advance had left the center thin, a weakness that Hitler sought to exploit. On August 2, 1944, Hitler condemned the *Westheer* to total defeat when he ordered the new commander of Army Group B, Field Marshal von Kluge, to launch a counteroffensive to retake Avranches and seal off the American breakout from Normandy. This decision was

a strategic blunder that completed the decimation of German forces in Normandy. Although the Germans hastily scraped together the elements of six, albeit much depleted, mechanized divisions, and built up supplies for a few days of sustained offensive action, this was insufficient for success.

Hans von Funck's XLVII Panzer Corps struck during the night of August 6–7 down the narrow corridor between the Sée and Sélune rivers toward Mortain and Avranches. Nonetheless, his troops were too depleted and tired, and von Funck had attacked prematurely before his forces could survey the ground. Moreover, on August 5 the Americans first detected a German buildup around Mortain, while eleventh-hour "Ultra" intercept intelligence warned of the enemy attack and allowed Bradley to undertake last-minute efforts to bolster his defenses.

American troops were still thin on the ground, occupied unprepared positions, and remained inexperienced at coordinating defensively. Nonetheless, American forces resolutely defended Hill 317, defying all German efforts to push through Mortain toward Avranches. Thereafter, the rapid arrival of American reserves quickly halted the offensive as Allied fighter-bombers disrupted the German drive through the *bocage* once the skies cleared on August 7. Indeed, the imbalance of forces was simply too great to allow a restabilization of the front and, logistically, the attack was doomed: the Germans had neither the firepower nor the supplies to recapture and hold Avranches.

The defeat of the Mortain counterattack presented the Allies with a strategic opportunity to encircle and destroy the German forces in Normandy, either in the Argentan–Falaise area or via a larger envelopment along the Seine River. With American forces advancing deep into their rear, the only feasible German strategy was to withdraw behind the Seine. Given the dire supply position and dwindling mobility, heavy losses were inevitable since the Mortain counterattack simply thrust the Germans farther into the noose of a pocket forming in the Argentan–Falaise area.

However, as American forces raced east to meet Montgomery's troops pushing south from Caen toward Falaise, they became strung out and short on supplies. Fearing overextension, friendly-fire casualties, and a successful German breakout amid a deteriorating supply situation, Bradley halted the American advance during August 13–18, divided his forces and directed V Corps to the Seine, which left neither thrust strong enough to defeat the enemy. The Americans had too little strength either to close the Falaise pocket at Argentan firmly from the south, or to push quickly north up both banks of the Seine after V Corps had established a bridgehead across the river at Mantes-Gassicourt on August 19. By going for a classic double encirclement, the Allies achieved neither objective.

Sluggish Anglo-Canadian progress contributed to the Allied failure to destroy the Germans in the Falaise pocket in mid-August. Although Crerar's newly operational Canadian First Army attacked south toward Argentan in two hastily organized offensives, Totalize and Tractable after August 8, a combination of inexperience and stubborn German resistance delayed the fall of Falaise until August 16. Lack of firm British pressure elsewhere allowed the enemy to conduct an orderly withdrawal from the pocket until August 19, when Canadian and Polish troops finally closed it. In the interim, 40,000 German troops had escaped.

Montgomery feared that his tired and depleted forces would suffer heavy losses and a possible setback if he tried to stop the desperate but determined enemy from escaping. Instead he, like Eisenhower, looked toward a larger envelopment along the Seine. At the same time, Montgomery underestimated the speed and mobility of the American forces; his refusal to alter the army group boundary to allow the Americans to advance past Argentan and close the pocket from the south contributed to Bradley's decision to halt the American advance on August 13.

It was therefore not until August 16 that Montgomery launched Operation Kitten, the long-planned advance to the Seine. Now the

Light Allied vehicles such as the one pictured here, had
relatively modest impact in the hard-slogging battles of June
and July, but once the German front collapsed in August, and
mobile operations ensued, they came into their own.
(Imperial War Museum, CL838)

On August 25, 1944, Allied troops – spearheaded by a French division – liberated Paris from German occupation. During the previous 48 hours, as the Germans prepared to withdraw from the city, French resistance fighters emerged from their places of hiding and commenced an armed uprising against their oppressors. (AKG Berlin)

Germans faced the prospect of a much larger encirclement on the Seine, as their dwindling mobility, catastrophic supply situation, and mounting demoralization presented the Allies with an opportunity to annihilate the enemy against the river. But after August 21 the Germans pulled off their greatest success of the campaign as they extricated virtually all of their remaining forces in a full-scale, staged withdrawal behind the Seine.

Changing strategic priorities, increasing demands for air support, and poor weather prevented Allied air forces from impeding the German retreat. Moreover, the Allied decision of August 18 to capture the Seine bridges intact then brought an end to direct attacks. The breakout also greatly increased the number of potential ground targets and inevitably dissipated Allied air power. Despite repeated air attacks and a catastrophic fuel situation, the Germans salvaged most of their troops and a surprising amount of equipment. They found no respite, however, as Allied forces rapidly advanced beyond the Seine. During the last week in August, therefore, the *Westheer* conducted a headlong

general withdrawal from France back toward the Belgian and German frontiers, closely pursued by Allied forces.

Continued retreat

During September 1–9, 1944, the *Westheer's* barely cohesive remnants could only slow the headlong Allied advance through France and Belgium. By September 10, however, this rapid Allied progress had outstripped a logistic network that had never been expected to support such a rate of advance. Consequently, difficulties in getting gasoline, munitions, and rations to the front slowed and then stalled Allied progress on a line that ran from the Belgian coast along the Meuse–Escaut canal to Maastricht, and then south from the German border at Aachen to the Swiss border near Belfort.

Reacting with customary German vigor, the *Westheer* seized this fleeting breathing space to rebuild its shattered cohesion. During September 6–12, for instance, the improvised Battle Group Chill assembled stragglers and local garrison forces to establish a fragile new defensive crust along the Meuse–Escaut canal. To fill the gap that had emerged in the German front between Antwerp and Neerpelt in Belgium, the High Command dispatched from the Reich part-trained army recruits, naval personnel, and air force ground crew to form General Kurt Student's improvised First

Parachute Army. Surprisingly, these partly trained and poorly equipped scratch units offered determined resistance.

A bitter dispute over both strategy and command had erupted between Eisenhower and Montgomery – the "broad front versus narrow front" controversy – in late August. On September 1, as planned before D-Day, Eisenhower – while continuing as Supreme Allied Commander – replaced Montgomery as Land Forces Commander in a theater that now deployed two American army groups in addition to Monty's Anglo-Canadian one. Failing to understand that American public opinion would not tolerate a British commander controlling a theater numerically dominated by the Americans, an insubordinate Montgomery campaigned to be reinstated as Land Forces Commander, or at least to be conceded powers of operational control over neighboring American forces.

Although this dispute did reflect Montgomery's egotism, his main motive was to shape the campaign according to the British army's partisan wishes. He desired that his limited British forces – while avoiding heavy casualties – should contribute significantly to Germany's military defeat, within a wider coalition, to secure Britain a strong voice in the postwar political environment. His coordination of neighboring American forces would allow his 21st Army Group – and thus Britain – to achieve a higher military profile than its limited resources would otherwise permit.

This issue of command was interconnected with a similar dispute over strategy. The politically sensitive Eisenhower wished to advance into Germany on a broad front, a strategy that held together the alliance by avoiding favoritism toward any national contingent. The forceful Montgomery, however, argued that his command – reinforced by American forces – should spearhead a concentrated blow north of the Ardennes against the key German Ruhr industrial zone. Displaying profound ignorance of wider political issues, Montgomery based his strategy on sound tactical logic, his own personality needs, and Britain's own interests within the wider multinational alliance. These two interlocked disputes rumbled on long into 1945, and soured Anglo-American relations during the rest of the campaign.

The V2

Germany's deployment of the V2 ballistic missile in the west during September 1944 forced Montgomery to launch his Market-Garden offensive to remove this threat. The Germans had begun developing this "vengeance" weapon back in 1940, and in early September 1944 German units in southwestern Holland fired their first missiles against Britain. Hitler hoped that these strikes would break British morale and serve as retaliation for the devastation that Allied strategic bombing had inflicted on the Reich. By the end of 1944, the Germans had fired 491 V2 missiles against British cities in a futile attempt to break Britain's will to fight.

During late 1944, the Germans employed the V2 missile more effectively, by launching 924 rockets – plus 1,000 V1 flying bombs – against Antwerp's harbor to disrupt the unloading of Allied supplies. Some 302 V-weapons hit the docks, destroying 60 ships and inflicting 15,000 casualties, many of them civilian. This sensible employment forced Montgomery to deploy 490 anti-aircraft guns around Antwerp to counter the V1 threat, though against the supersonic V2 the Allies remained helpless.

By early 1945, however, the deteriorating strategic situation and supply shortages were hampering the Germans' use of the V2. Overall, the strategic impact of this supposed war-winning "wonder weapon" was hugely disappointing, especially given the enormous resources devoted to its development – ones that Germany could have used more effectively, for example, to produce additional tanks, jet aircraft, submarines and flak guns.

Market-Garden

During early September 1944, Montgomery sought to rebuild Allied momentum, lost due to supply problems, before the *Westheer* recovered its cohesion. He hoped to quickly secure both the enemy's V2 launch sites and an intact bridge over the Rhine River, and to use the latter success to secure from Eisenhower priority in the allocation of supplies for a British-led "narrow-thrust" against the Ruhr. Consequently, on September 17, Montgomery initiated Operation Market-Garden, an atypically audacious combined ground and airborne offensive.

Operation Market-Garden, September 17–26, 1944

1. Colonel Frost's 2nd Parachute Battalion heroically holds northern end of Arnhem bridge September 17–21 until overwhelmed by numerically superior forces.
2. Remnants of 1st (British) Airborne Division withdraws from Oosterbeek perimeter, night September 25–26.

0 _____ 25 miles
0 _____ 25 km

Allied front line on September 17, 1944
Allied front line on September 26, 1944
Allied airborne forces landing zones
Allied intended advance
Waffen-SS

One motive for this sudden audacity was Montgomery's recognition that early September 1944 offered a fleeting opportunity for the 21st Army Group to achieve his partisan British objectives in the theater. With the *Westheer* brought to its knees, one daring, final, all-out British effort could secure for Britain a high profile within the wider Allied defeat of Germany. If the war dragged on into 1945, however, increasing American numerical domination of the campaign would further erode Britain's declining strategic influence.

Market-Garden envisaged General Brian Horrocks' XXX British Corps thrusting swiftly north through Holland to link up with some 30,000 British and American airborne troops landed at key river bridges and crossroads along the way to facilitate the ground advance. At the northern drop zone, the British 1st Airborne Division was to seize Arnhem bridge and hold it until Horrocks' armor arrived. The offensive soon

Although Lieutenant-Colonel John Frost's encircled British paratroopers resisted heroically at Arnhem bridge for six days, overwhelmingly powerful German attacks finally crushed them before the armor of Horrocks' XXX Corps could advance north to reach them. (Imperial War Museum MH 2062)

encountered difficulties, however, as the desperate defensive improvisations enacted by Field Marshal Walther Model – the new commander of Army Group B – slowed Horrocks' ground advance. To make matters worse, local German counterattacks threatened Horrocks' flanks and even temporarily cut off the flow of supplies to his spearheads. Meanwhile, hastily mobilized garrison forces, stiffened by the remnants of the crack II SS Panzer Corps and reinforced with King Tiger tanks, steadily wore down the heroic resistance offered by Colonel Frost's paratroopers at Arnhem bridge, while simultaneously containing the rest of the 1st Airborne Division in the Oosterbeek perimeter to the west of Arnhem.

After five days' resistance, and without sign of relief by Horrocks' forces, the Germans overran Frost's forces at the bridge. Within a few days, further German pressure had also forced the remnants of the 1st Airborne Division to withdraw from Oosterbeek to the south bank of the lower Rhine. Although Market-Garden was an expensive failure – despite the justification that Montgomery tried to offer for this operation – the capture of the Waal River bridge at Nijmegen proved strategically vital, for it was from here that Montgomery launched his February 1945 Veritable offensive toward the Rhine River. Moreover, the British commander drew the correct

The distinctive "Dragon's Teeth" anti-tank obstacles became the characteristic image of Hitler's last fortified position in the west – the Siegfried Line or West Wall. Although the line held up the Allies in places, as well as inflicting heavy casualties upon them, it could not alter Germany's inevitable demise. By early 1945, the Allies had breached the entire Siegfried Line and were pushing the Germans back to the Rhine River. (Imperial War Museum EA 37737)

conclusion from Market-Garden – that even a weakened *Westheer* could still inflict a dangerous reverse on overly ambitious Allied offensive actions.

As Market-Garden was unfolding, Bradley's 12th US Army Group, deployed along the Sittard–Epinal sector, continued its modest eastward progress to initiate the first assaults on the West Wall – the German fortifications along the Reich's western border, known to the Allies as the Siegfried Line. Although supply shortages prevented much of Hodges' First US Army from attacking, the remainder did thrust east to capture Sittard and assault the Siegfried Line near Aachen. Farther south, General Patton's Third US Army pushed east 50 miles (80 km) to cross the Upper Moselle valley and close on the fortified town of Metz.

Between September 13 and October 21, 1944, it took repeated American assaults to capture Aachen against ferocious German resistance. Protected by the Siegfried Line, the defenders fought tenaciously for this

It took the Americans five weeks of heavy attritional fighting to overcome determined German resistance in the historic city of Aachen: but after its surrender columns of German prisoners streamed west into captivity. (AKG Berlin)

historic city that Hitler had decreed would be held to the last man and bullet. To boost German defensive resilience, military police roamed the rear areas summarily hanging alleged shirkers from trees to encourage the others. Spurred on by such threats and by the need to protect the Reich, the outnumbered defenders resisted vigorously and even launched local counterthrusts against American advances. The few German fighter-bombers available ran the gauntlet of Allied aerial supremacy to strafe the advancing enemy.

Despite these desperate efforts, American determination and numerical superiority eventually told, and on October 21 Aachen

fell. The Western Allies had penetrated the much-feared Siegfried Line and captured their first German city. Nevertheless, the considerable time and high casualties incurred in achieving this local success both concerned the Americans and led them to abandon launching individual narrow thrusts against the Siegfried Line.

Clearing the Scheldt

Between mid-September and early November 1944, the First Canadian Army – now temporarily led by Lieutenant-General Guy Simonds in place of the sick General Henry Crerar – struggled to capture the Scheldt estuary in southwestern Holland in the face of fierce enemy resistance. The Germans had managed to establish a solid front in Zeeland – along South Beveland, around Breskens, and on Walcheren island – by extricating the

During September 4–6, 1944, General von Zangen's Fifteenth Army used all manner of vessels – including fishing boats such as these – to mount an improvised evacuation north across the Scheldt estuary to the Breskens area. This successful withdrawal enabled the Germans to hold onto the Scheldt estuary, thus denying the Allies use of the vital port of Antwerp until early November. (Imperial War Museum)

Fifteenth Army from potential encirclement south of the Scheldt estuary. During September 4–26, this army used improvised boats and rafts to evacuate 86,000 troops and 616 guns north across the estuary.

Most of the Western Allies' supplies were still being landed at the precarious facilities established on Normandy's beaches. This continuing logistic reliance on the original beachheads owed much to Hitler's orders that the German garrisons encircled at French and Belgian ports continue resisting to prevent the Allies from using these harbors. The Allies needed to clear the Scheldt estuary rapidly so that they could land supplies at the port of Antwerp, captured by Horrocks' forces on September 4. Therefore, between September 5 and October 1, to secure their rear areas as a prelude to clearing the Scheldt, the

Canadians captured the ports of Le Havre, Boulogne, and Calais.

Unfortunately for the Allies, it took Simonds' understrength army until early November to complete its clearance of the Scheldt. The slow Canadian advance owed much to shortages of resources because Montgomery – despite recognizing the importance of Antwerp's docks – had awarded logistical priority to Dempsey's command for Market-Garden. In addition, the difficult terrain, which assisted a skillful improvised German defense, slowed the Canadians. During October 2–16, Simonds' forces advanced north to capture Bergen-op-Zoom and seal off the South Beveland peninsula. The German defense here cleverly utilized the terrain, by constructing bunkers in the steep rear slopes of the area's numerous raised dikes, and locating rocket-launchers immediately behind them. The Allies soon learned how hard it was to neutralize these positions.

Meanwhile, between October 6 and November 3, in Operation Switchback, the Canadians also cleared German resistance in the Breskens pocket south of the Scheldt, after previous Allied attacks in mid-September had been repulsed. Here, the Germans deliberately flooded the Leopold Canal to channel the Canadians onto the area's few raised dike-roads, which the defenders had turned into pre-surveyed killing zones covered by artillery, anti-tank guns, and rocket-launchers. The Canadians had to combine effective artillery support with determination to secure the Breskens pocket in the face of such fierce resistance.

Between October 16 and November 1, 1944, Simonds' forces also advanced west along South Beveland and then prepared to launch an amphibious assault on the German fortress-island of Walcheren. This attack was made possible by an audacious plan – for, at Simonds' insistence, during October 3–17, five Allied bombing strikes breached the sea-dike that surrounded Walcheren. Through these breaches the sea poured to flood the island's low-lying center,

The culminating point of the First Canadian's Army slogging battles to secure the Scheldt estuary was its assault on the heavily fortified German-held island of Walcheren. To overcome the powerful enemy defenses without incurring heavy casualties, Allied strategic bombers destroyed sections of the island's perimeter dikes, allowing the sea to pour in to flood the low-lying center of the island. (Imperial War Museum C4668)

eliminating 11 of the enemy's 28 artillery batteries. Then, during November 1–7, in Operation Infatuate, two amphibious assaults backed by a land attack from South Beveland secured the flooded fortress.

Thus, by November 7 the First Canadian Army had successfully cleared the Germans from the Scheldt, but this slogging effort in difficult terrain had cost them 13,000 casualties and had taken no fewer than nine weeks. This sobering experience underscored the Allied high command's belief – derived from the attack on Aachen – that pushing deep into the Reich would prove a difficult task.

During mid-October, while the Scheldt battles raged along Montgomery's western flank, the German forces facing Dempsey's army strengthened their defenses and the British sought to gain better positions for future attacks. Then, out of the blue, during the night of October 26–27, 1944, two German mechanized divisions struck Dempsey's thinly held positions at Meijel, in the Peel marshes southeast of Eindhoven, in a local riposte. Although the Germans initially made progress, Dempsey moved up reinforcements, including massed artillery, and then, between October 29 and November 7, drove the Germans back to their original positions.

Despite its inevitable failure, the German attack on Meijel demonstrated to the Western Allies that, notwithstanding the disasters that the *Westheer* had suffered in Normandy, it could still mount a surprise counterstrike against weakly defended sections of the Allied line. Equally, though, the riposte also showed the Germans how unlikely such counterattacks were to succeed, once Allied numerical superiority was brought to bear. The initial success of Hitler's surprise mid-December 1944 Ardennes counterattack showed that the Western Allies had not learned the lessons of Meijel; equally, though, the inevitable demise of the Ardennes offensive showed that the Germans had not learned them either.

On November 2, 1944, Eisenhower issued new strategic directives for the campaign. While Devers' and Bradley's commands were to push east to secure bridgeheads over the Rhine in subsidiary actions, Montgomery's army group was to launch the Allied main effort with a strike across the Rhine to surround the Ruhr. As a preliminary to such an offensive, between November 14 and December 4, Dempsey's army – despite waterlogged conditions – thrust east to clear the west bank of the Meuse River around Venlo. Simultaneously, Simpson's Ninth US Army – now returned to Bradley after serving under Montgomery – and Hodges' First US Army resumed their push through the Siegfried Line toward Jülich and Monschau between November 16 and December 15.

Although American forces reached the Roer River between Linnich and Düren, VII and V US Corps became locked in bitter fighting in the difficult terrain of the Hürtgen Forest. Unfortunately for Eisenhower, V Corps, in the face of bitter local counterthrusts, failed to capture the key Schwammenauel Dam that dominated the entire Roer valley. Meanwhile, to protect Simpson's northern flank, the British XXX Corps struck east during November 18–22 to capture Geilenkirchen, before the assault stalled due to saturated ground. This left a German salient that jutted west of the Roer River around

Heinsberg, and Montgomery – who always desired a "tidy" front line – wanted to clear it before striking farther east. But just as British forces prepared to launch Operation Blackcock to secure this area, the German Ardennes counteroffensive erupted.

Further south, on November 8, Patton's Third US Army resumed its battering assaults on the fortress-city of Metz, but ammunition shortages so hampered these attacks that the town did not fall until November 22. Elsewhere, Patton's forces – despite continuing supply shortages – made more rapid progress, and by December 6 had secured bridgeheads over the Roer River and penetrated into the Siegfried Line at Saarlautern.

To Patton's south, the offensive initiated by Devers' 6th US Army Group on November 13, made even swifter progress. By November 23, Lieutenant-General Alexander Patch's Seventh US Army had captured Strasbourg, and over the next 14 days it fanned out to reach the Rhine River on a 50-mile (80 km) front. Farther south, the seven divisions of General Jean de Lattre de Tassigny's First French Army thrust east through Belfort to reach the Rhine River just north of the German–Swiss border by November 20. These hard-won advances, which cost Devers' command 28,000 casualties, left a German salient that jutted west beyond the Rhine at Colmar. Yet just as these various Western Allied operations, designed to reach the Rhine and secure bridgeheads over it, neared fruition, the *Westheer* rudely shattered the growing aura of Allied confidence with an unexpected counterblow.

The Battle of the Bulge

As early as September 16, 1944, Hitler had decided to stage a counteroffensive in the west that would seize the strategic initiative and alter decisively the course of the campaign. Hitler hoped to seize the key port of Antwerp by a surprise strike through the Ardennes, despite the unfavorable battlefield situation. Well aware that Allied aerial superiority hampered their mobility, however, the Germans decided to attack only during a predicted period of lengthy bad weather that would ground the powerful Allied tactical air forces.

During October and November the Germans prepared frantically for the attack – now planned to begin in mid-December – while covering their activities with sophisticated deceptions. These preparations included rebuilding the seven shattered panzer divisions slated to spearhead the operation, as well as augmenting German infantry strength with 12 *Volksgrenadier* (People's Infantry) Divisions, recently mobilized by throwing together ex-naval recruits, air force ground crew, and convalescents.

The Germans earmarked the three armies of Model's Army Group B for the offensive, with SS Colonel-General Josef Dietrich's Sixth Panzer Army and General Hasso von Manteuffel's Fifth Panzer Army spearheading the operation in the northern and central sectors, respectively; the weaker Seventh Army was merely to secure the southern flank. Excluding reserves, this force amounted to eight mechanized and 14 infantry divisions with 950 AFVs.

The intended German battle zone was the hilly, stream-bisected, and forested terrain of the Ardennes, since this region's unsuitability for armored warfare had led the Americans to defend it with just four divisions. Consequently, the Ardennes offered the German attack the prospect of local success, despite its unsuitable terrain. Hitler, however, gambled on an ambitious strategic victory by seeking to capture Antwerp, 95 miles (153 km) away, to cut off Montgomery's command from the American forces deployed to his south.

Despite the frenetic German preparations, the attack's objective was too ambitious relative to the modest force assembled and the vast resources on which the Western Allies could call. Indeed, many German commanders argued that their forces were too weak to seize Antwerp, but Hitler remained obdurate. The greatest flaw in the Germans' plan was that their logistical base remained utterly inadequate to support such a grandiose attack. The German forces remained short of fuel, and some commanders planned to utilize captured Allied fuel stocks to sustain the offensive. At Hitler's insistence – and contrary to his senior commanders' professional advice – the *Westheer* risked its last precious armored reserves on the triumph that might be achieved by a barely sustainable surprise blow against this Allied weak spot. Hitler failed to consider the consequences that would accrue if the gamble failed.

The Germans did everything in their power to improve their slim chances of success, with Dietrich, for example, employing his *Volksgrenadier* divisions to conduct the initial break-in, and saving the armor for the exploitation phase deep into the Allied rear. Furthermore, the Germans employed SS Colonel Otto Skorzeny's commandos – some dressed as American Military Police – to infiltrate behind the Allied lines to spread confusion and help sustain offensive momentum. Although the Germans gained some advantages from this ruse, the operation failed to significantly hamper Allied reactions.

Before dawn on December 16, 1944, the *Volksgrenadiers* of Sixth Panzer Army broke into the Allied defenses before I SS Panzer Corps struck west toward the Meuse bridges south of Liège. SS Lieutenant-Colonel Joachim Peiper's armored battle group spearheaded the corps advance with a mixed force of Panzer IV and Panther tanks, plus 30 lumbering King Tigers that did their best to keep up. Peiper's mission was to exploit ruthlessly any success with a rapid drive toward Antwerp before the Allies could react. Given Peiper's mission and the terrain, his King Tigers played only a minor role in the offensive – contrary to popular perception, which regards this operation as being dominated by these leviathans.

During December 18–19, Peiper's force stalled at Stoumont because the Americans had destroyed the few available river bridges in the area, and flanking forces had failed to

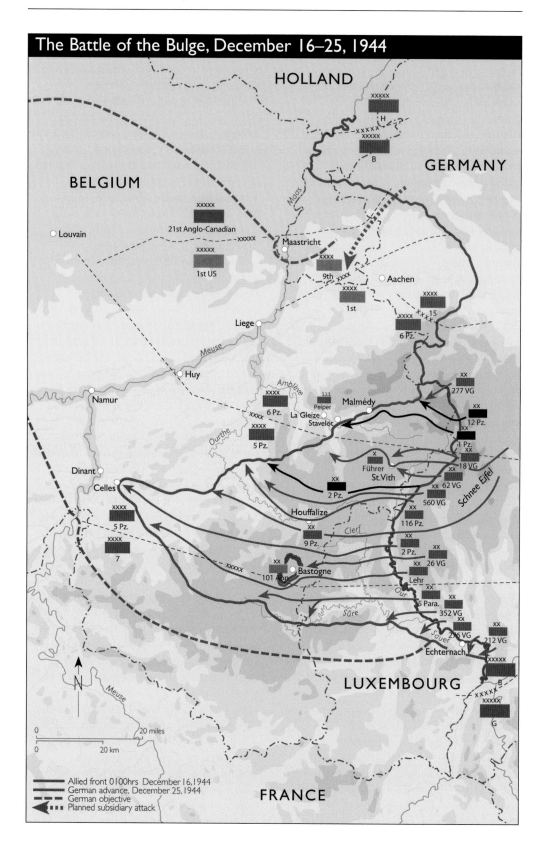

The Battle of the Bulge, December 16–25, 1944

HOLLAND

GERMANY

BELGIUM

Maas

Louvain

21st Anglo-Canadian

XXXXX

Maastricht

1st US

XXXXX

9th

Aachen

1st

15

6 Pz.

Liege

Meuse

Huy

Amblève

Namur

6 Pz.

Peiper

Malmédy

277 VG

La Gleize

Stavelot

12 Pz.

5 Pz.

1 Pz.

Ourthe

Führer

18 VG

Dinant

St. Vith

Celles

2 Pz.

62 VG

560 VG

Houffalize

116 Pz.

5 Pz.

9 Pz.

Clerf

2 Pz.

7

26 VG

Bastogne

Lehr

101 Abn

Our

5 Para.

352 VG

Sûre

276 VG

212 VG

Schnee Eifel

Sauer

Echternach

LUXEMBOURG

N

Meuse

0   20 miles

0   20 km

Allied front 0100hrs December 16, 1944
German advance, December 25, 1944
German objective
Planned subsidiary attack

FRANCE

protect Peiper's supply lines. During this advance, Peiper's SS fanatics had murdered 77 American prisoners at Malmédy, plus 120 Belgian civilians in numerous separate incidents. By December 22, Allied counterstrikes – supported by fighter-bombers after the mist that had kept them grounded over the previous six days lifted – had surrounded Peiper's forces at La Gleize.

During the night of December 23–24, Peiper's doomed unit – now out of fuel and munitions – destroyed its vehicles, and the remaining 800 unwounded soldiers exfiltrated on foot back to the German lines. The destruction of Peiper's group forced Dietrich on December 22 to commit II SS Panzer Corps to rescue the collapsing northern thrust, but by December 26 this too had stalled near Manhay. Overall, the thrust undertaken by Dietrich's army had proved a costly failure.

On December 16, to Dietrich's south, the Fifth Panzer Army also struck the unsuspecting Allied front. Although fierce American resistance at St. Vith slowed von Manteuffel's infantry thrusts during December 16–17, farther south his two spearhead panzer corps advanced 20 miles (32 km) toward Houffalize and Bastogne. During December 18–22, these corps surrounded the American 101st Airborne Division at Bastogne and pushed farther west to within just 4 miles (6.4 km) of the vital Meuse bridges. When the Germans invited the commander of the surrounded Bastogne garrison to surrender, he tersely replied: "Nuts!" After this rebuff the initiative slowly slipped out of the Germans' grasp thanks to fierce American resistance, rapid commitment of substantial Allied reserves, and severe German logistic shortages.

The Americans commenced their counterattacks on December 23, driving northeast to relieve Bastogne on December 26, and forcing back the German spearheads near the Meuse. Even though Field Marshal von Rundstedt, Commander-in-Chief West, now concluded that the operation had failed, the Führer nevertheless insisted that one more effort be made to

penetrate the Allied defenses. Consequently, on New Year's Day 1945, von Manteuffel's army initiated new attacks near Bastogne.

To help this last-gasp attempt to snatch success from the jaws of defeat, the *Westheer* initiated a diversionary attack, Operation Northwind, in Alsace-Lorraine on New Year's Eve 1944. The Germans intended that a thrust north from the Colmar pocket – the German-held salient that jutted west over the Rhine into France – would link up at Strasbourg with a six-division attack south from the Saar. Although Hitler hoped that the attack would divert enemy reinforcements away from the Ardennes, in reality Northwind incurred heavy losses, yet only secured modest success and sucked few forces away from "the Bulge."

Consequently, the renewed German Ardennes attack soon stalled in the face of increasing Allied strength. Finally, on January 3, 1945, Allied forces struck the northern and southern flanks of the German salient to squeeze it into extinction. Over the next 13 days, instead of immediately retreating, the *Westheer* – at Hitler's insistence – conducted a costly fighting withdrawal back to its original position.

Just one self-inflicted injury marred the strategic triumph secured by the Allies in the Ardennes. As the German advance hampered Bradley's control of the First and Ninth US Armies in his northern sector, Eisenhower acquiesced to Monty's demands and placed these forces under his control. Although the commitment of the British XXX Corps had helped the Allied victory, the Ardennes was essentially an American triumph. Unfortunately, on January 7, 1945, in a press conference Montgomery claimed credit for this victory, thus souring Anglo-American relations for the rest of the campaign.

During the four-week Battle of the Bulge, Model's command lost 120,000 troops and 600 precious AFVs. By mid-January 1945, therefore, only weak German forces now stood between the Allies and a successful advance across the Rhine into the Reich. With hindsight, the Ardennes counterstrike represented one of Hitler's gravest strategic errors. It was a futile, costly, and strategically disastrous gamble that tossed away Germany's last armored reserves. Moreover, the Germans managed to assemble sufficient forces for the counterstrike only by starving the Eastern Front of much-needed reinforcements. Consequently, when the Soviets resumed their offensives in mid-January 1945, they easily smashed through the German front in Poland. By late January, therefore, these German defeats on both the Eastern and Western Fronts ensured that it would only be a matter of months before the Nazi Reich succumbed.

The Western Allies, having by January 15, 1945, restored the mid-December 1944 front line, exploited this success with further offensives. The next day, Dempsey's XII Corps commenced its Blackcock offensive to clear the enemy's salient west of the Roer River around Heinsberg. Hampered both by poor weather, which grounded Allied tactical air power, and by stiff German resistance, XII Corps struggled forward until by January 26 the Allies held a continuous line along the Roer from Roermond down to Schmidt. Then, on January 20, the First French Army attacked the Colmar salient south of Strasbourg.

The defenders, General Rasp's Nineteenth Army, formed part of the recently raised Army Group Upper Rhine, which was led not by a professional officer but by the Reichsführer-SS, Heinrich Himmler. Unsurprisingly, given Himmler's military inexperience and the losses incurred in Northwind, the French made steady progress, but Hitler equally predictably forbade Rasp from withdrawing. Under pressure, however, Hitler freed Rasp from his chief handicap – he dissolved Himmler's command, subordinated its forces to the more professional control of Army Group G, and brought in the experienced Paul Hausser to lead this command.

Rasp, however, soon realized that these measures could not prevent his forces from being destroyed if they obeyed Hitler's prohibition on retreat. To save his remaining troops, Rasp disobeyed his Führer and withdrew them back across the Rhine, thus saving precious forces with which to defend this last major obstacle before the heart of the Reich. By February 9, the First French Army held the entire left bank of the upper Rhine.

By early February 1945, the Western Allies were ready to initiate further offensives to secure the remainder of the Rhine's western bank. Hitler, however, now convinced himself that the Allies had temporarily exhausted their offensive power, and so transferred Dietrich's Sixth Panzer Army from the west to the Eastern Front. Yet the Führer did not send this force to Poland, where it was sorely needed to stop the rapidly advancing Soviets, but instead to Hungary for a futile offensive to relieve encircled Budapest.

By now, the Western Allies outnumbered von Rundstedt's three army groups by four to one in manpower and eight to one in armor. In the north, General Johannes Blaskowitz's Army Group H held the front facing Monty's command from Rotterdam through to Roermond, including the vital Reichswald Forest manned by Lieutenant-General Alfred Schlemm's First Parachute Army. Model's Army Group B faced Bradley's forces in the Rhineland from Roermond south to Trier. Finally, Hausser's Army Group G held the front from the Saarland down to the Swiss border against Devers' divisions.

The *Westheer* hoped first to slow the Allied advance through the Siegfried Line, and then gradually retreat back to the Rhine, and there use this obstacle to halt permanently the Allied advance. Hitler, though, again forbade any retreat and insisted that the outnumbered *Westheer* hold the Allies at the Siegfried Line. To retreat back to the Rhine, Hitler argued, would simply transfer the impending catastrophe from one geographical location to another.

On February 8, 1945, Montgomery's forces commenced Operation Veritable, the great offensive for which they had been preparing when the German Ardennes counterattack broke. The reinforced British XXX Corps – now part of Crerar's First Canadian Army –

struck Schlemm's First Parachute Army in its Siegfried Line defenses between Nijmegen and Mook. The offensive sought to drive the Germans back across the Rhine around Wesel to permit a subsequent thrust deep into the Reich. After an intense 1,050-gun artillery bombardment, three British and two Canadian infantry divisions broke into the German defenses. Despite significant Allied numerical superiority, the poor terrain of the Reichswald Forest in the south and the deliberate German flooding of the low-lying Rhine flood-plain in the north, slowed the Canadian advance east.

The Germans also released water from the Schwammenauel Dam to flood the Roer valley on February 9. This prevented Simpson's Ninth US Army – again temporarily under Monty's command – from initiating its own Grenade offensive toward the Rhine on February 10. Montgomery intended that Veritable and Grenade would form the northern and southern pincers of a simultaneous double encirclement designed to link up at Wesel on the Rhine. Despite knowing that the flooding had delayed Grenade for 10 days, Montgomery nevertheless continued Veritable after February 10 as planned, because by sucking German reserves to the British thrust, he reasoned, the Ninth US Army would advance more rapidly to Wesel.

Despite penetrating the Siegfried Line, Crerar's forces – now reinforced by II Canadian Corps – made only slow progress. The combination of fierce enemy resistance by newly arrived reserves and the Germans' advantage of defending from their Hochwald Layback defenses, together with poor weather and saturated terrain, all slowed the Allied advance. Nevertheless, Montgomery relentlessly kept the offensive driving east, grinding down the enemy until by February 28 they had been forced back to a small bridgehead west of the Rhine at Wesel. While officially still forbidding any withdrawals, Hitler now realized that the *Westheer* could not hold the Allies west of the Rhine. Consequently, he ordered that any commander who demolished a Rhine

bridge too early – thus preventing retreating German forces from crossing – or who allowed a bridge to fall into enemy hands would be shot. This contradictory order would cause the Germans untold problems on March 7 at Remagen.

Finally, on February 23, the Americans commenced Grenade across the now subsiding Roer River. As Montgomery expected, these forces made rapid progress toward Wesel as Veritable had already sucked German reserves north, and by March 3 the Americans and British had linked up at Geldern. During March 8–10, Schlemm – with the connivance of von Blaskowitz – disobeyed Hitler by withdrawing his remaining forces across the Rhine at Wesel before destroying the remaining two bridges. Veritable had cost the 21st Army Group 23,000 casualties in four weeks of bitter, attritional, fighting against the resolute defense that Schlemm had orchestrated. It was only Hitler's grudging acceptance of this fact that allowed Schlemm to avoid execution for his disobedience.

Crossing the Rhine

To the south of Grenade, Hodges' First US Army – part of Bradley's command – commenced an attack across the subsiding Roer River on February 23, 1945, that sought to reach the Rhine between Düsseldorf and Cologne. Meanwhile, Patton's Third US Army thrust toward Trier and the River Kyll, and by March 1 had secured both objectives. After Eisenhower's March 3 strategic directive, Bradley's command expanded these attacks into a drive toward the Rhine between Düsseldorf and Koblenz. By March 9, the First US Army had reached these objectives and linked up with Simpson's forces near Düsseldorf.

Despite the rapidity of Hodges' advance toward the Rhine, the Germans nevertheless managed to demolish all of the Rhine bridges in this sector – except the Ludendorff railway bridge at Remagen, between Cologne and Koblenz. In a fatal blow to Hitler's hopes, on March 7, Hodges' forces captured

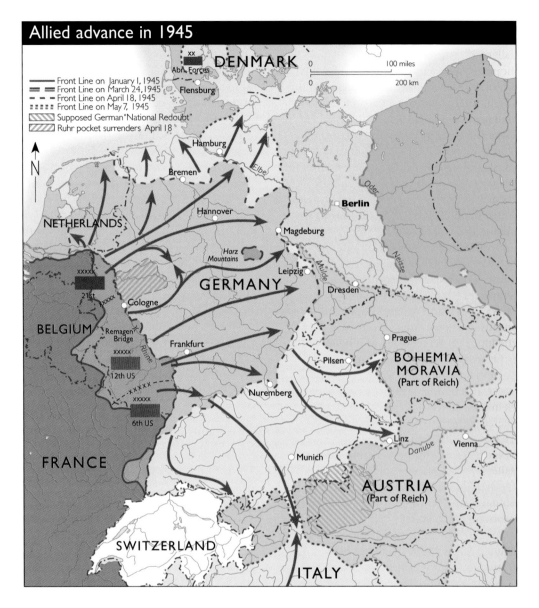

Allied advance in 1945

Front Line on January 1, 1945
Front Line on March 24, 1945
Front Line on April 18, 1945
Front Line on May 7, 1945
Supposed German "National Redoubt"
Ruhr pocket surrenders April 18

DENMARK
Abn. Forces
Flensburg
Hamburg
Bremen
Elbe
Berlin
Oder
Hannover
Magdeburg
NETHERLANDS
Harz Mountains
Neisse
Leipzig
GERMANY
Mulde
Dresden
21st
XXXXX
Cologne
BELGIUM
Remagen Bridge
Frankfurt
Rhine
Prague
Pilsen
BOHEMIA-MORAVIA
(Part of Reich)
12th US
XXXXX
XXXXX
Nuremberg
6th US
XXXXX
Linz
Danube
Vienna
FRANCE
Munich
AUSTRIA
(Part of Reich)
SWITZERLAND
ITALY

0   100 miles
0   200 km

N

the badly damaged – but still intact –
Remagen bridge. Recognizing the
opportunity that this good fortune offered,
Hodges daringly pushed reinforcements
across the river to enlarge the bridgehead
before the Germans could throw in whatever
reserves they had available.

At Remagen on March 6, with the
Americans rapidly approaching the
Ludendorff bridge, the garrison commander
understandably was anxious. If the enemy
captured the bridge, he faced execution; if he
blew up the bridge too soon, trapping

German forces on the west bank, he faced
execution. The commander decided not to
blow up the structure until the next morning
to allow friendly forces to cross, but
unexpectedly American armor – spearheaded
by the powerful new Pershing tank –
appeared and stormed the bridge. The
Germans triggered their demolition charges,
which failed to explode, and then ignited
the backup charges, which exploded but
only damaged the bridge instead of
destroying it. Within hours, substantial
American forces had crossed the river and

established a bridgehead on the eastern bank. The elusive intact Rhine bridge had fallen into Patton's hands, and the *Westheer's* hopes of stopping the Western Allies at the Rhine had been shattered.

Hitler reacted furiously to the loss of the Remagen bridge: he ordered that seven German officers be executed, and sacked von Rundstedt as Commander-in-Chief West. In his place, the Führer appointed Field Marshal Albert Kesselring, transferred from the Italian front. On his arrival, Kesselring mocked the German propaganda that promised the imminent arrival of new war-winning weapons, by stating that he was the long-awaited V3! Predictably, Kesselring's arrival exerted as minimal an impact on the Allied advance as had the two previous German V-weapons. Subsequently, during March 8–16, as the Americans gradually expanded the Remagen bridgehead, the Germans in vain attempted to destroy the bridge through aerial, V2 rocket, and artillery strikes. The severely damaged bridge eventually collapsed on March 17, but by then it was too late: Hodges' forces had already constructed several pontoon bridges alongside the now fallen structure.

On March 8, 1945, Eisenhower's new strategic directive confirmed that Montgomery's command would attack across the Rhine near Wesel in Operation Plunder, and issued new orders for both the 12th and 6th US Amy Groups. On that day the XII Corps of Patton's Third US Army had linked up with Hodges' forces in the Remagen–Koblenz area to encircle 50,000 German soldiers north of the Eifel ridge. Eisenhower now instructed Patton's army to drive southeast across the Moselle River into the Saar industrial region toward Mannheim. Here they were to link up with the northeasterly advance of Patch's Seventh US Army, part of Devers' 6th Army Group, through the Siegfried Line from Saarbrücken. The final objective of Patton and Patch's commands was to secure a continuous front along the Rhine from Koblenz to Karlsruhe.

On March 9, Patton's XII US Corps swung south and, having crossed the Moselle, struck southeast through the Hunsrück mountains toward Bingen on the confluence of the Nahe and Rhine rivers. Then on March 13, Walker's XX Corps thrust east from Trier through the Saar–Palatinate to link up with XII Corps on the Nahe near Bad Kreuzbach and encircle elements of the German Seventh Army. Last, on March 15, Patch's Seventh US Army struck northeast from Saarbrücken, aiming to link up with Patton's two corps between Mainz and Mannheim, and to encircle General Förtsch's First Army. As these pincers closed, SS Colonel-General Paul Hausser – recognizing the calamity about to engulf his Army Group G – in vain begged Hitler for permission to withdraw east of the Rhine. By March 24, Patton and Patch's forces had linked up near Mannheim and successfully surrounded most of Förtsch's disintegrating army. Together these operations inflicted 113,000 casualties on the enemy, including 90,000 prisoners, for the cost of 18,000 American losses.

Then, on March 22, Patton's forces launched a surprise amphibious assault across the Rhine at Oppenheim, between Mainz and Mannheim, and within 72 hours had established a firm salient east of the river. The Americans now possessed two toeholds across the Rhine, whereas in the north along the supposed Allied main axis, the cautious Montgomery was still readying himself for a massive strike across the river at Wesel. Overall, these hard-fought offensives to clear the west bank of the Rhine, conducted by five Allied armies between February 10 and March 23, 1945, had secured 280,000 German prisoners, for the cost of 96,000 Allied casualties.

Predictably, the Führer reacted to these disasters with increasingly desperate measures to slow the enemy advance. On March 19, Hitler – in a drastic scorched earth policy – ordered the destruction of anything that the Allies might find of value. By failing to hold back the enemy, Hitler reasoned, the German people had demonstrated their racial weaknesses, and thus had forfeited the right to save their homeland from the cataclysm Hitler now intended to unleash on Germany in a bid to stem the Allied advance. Fortunately for Germany, in the chaos that now pervaded the collapsing Reich, the Minister of War Production, Albert Speer, sabotaged Hitler's intent to plunge the country into an orgy of self-inflicted destruction.

Operation Plunder

During March 1945, as the Americans cleared the Saar–Palatinate and established two bridgeheads east of the Rhine, Montgomery continued building up overwhelming resources for his planned offensive to cross the Rhine around Wesel. The once formidable German First Parachute Army manned this key sector, but its 13 divisions now mustered just 45 tanks and 69,000 weary troops. During the night of March 23–24, the 21st Army Group – still augmented by Ninth US Army – commenced its attack with massive artillery and aerial strikes. This was followed by an amphibious assault across the Rhine along a 20-mile (32 km) front, code-named Plunder, while simultaneously in Varsity two airborne divisions landed behind the German front to shatter its cohesion. The Germans, however, had anticipated an airborne assault and had redeployed many flak guns from the Ruhr, and these downed 105 Allied aircraft.

Despite this, the British had learned from the mistakes made during Market-Garden, and the proximity of the landing zones to the main front ensured that the ground advance linked up with the airborne forces during March 24. Despite fierce resistance by German paratroopers that delayed XXX British Corps, by dusk on March 24 the Allied bridgehead was already 5 miles (8 km) deep. Yet it took another four days' consolidation of the bridgehead before the cautious Monty declared that the struggle for the Rhine had been successful.

By this time, in addition to the Remagen and Oppenheim bridgeheads, Bradley's and

Devers' forces had also secured two further crossings of the Rhine. Now, with German units virtually immobilized by lack of fuel and by Allied air power, as well as hampered by chronic equipment shortages, the battered *Westheer* began to disintegrate. To resist the Western Allies' 74 well-equipped divisions, the Germans could now field – even including its Home Guard militia – the equivalent of just 27 full-strength divisions.

After late March, the Western Allies pushed rapidly east beyond the Rhine into the heart of Germany to link up with the westward Soviet advance and thus defeat Hitler's Reich. Prior to March 28, Eisenhower's strategic intent had been to advance toward Berlin. Yet now, in the final twist of the protracted dispute between him and Montgomery, he shifted the point of main effort to Bradley's planned thrust toward the Elbe River. In so doing, Eisenhower denied Montgomery the glorious, British-dominated, victory the latter so fervently desired.

Then, on March 28, Dempsey's Second (British) Army broke out from its Rhine bridgehead at Wesel with the intent to clear northern Germany and link up with the Soviets on the Baltic coast near Wismar. Against weak resistance, three British corps made rapid progress and by April 8 had advanced 118 miles (189 km) to cross the River Weser southeast of Bremen. Simultaneously, to protect the British left flank, II Canadian Corps struck north from Emmerich and advanced 69 miles (111 km) to seize Coevorden in Holland. To slow the British drive east, a desperate Hitler re-appointed his former favorite – the now disgraced General Student – to command the First Parachute Army. Yet by now the strategic situation had so deteriorated that Hitler's arch sycophant – the Armed Forces Chief of Staff Colonel-General Alfred Jodl – could tell his Führer that even the employment of a dozen military geniuses like Student would not prevent Germany's inevitable demise.

During late March 1945, to Monty's south, Bradley commenced attacks to secure

Field Marshal Walther Model, seen here early in the war, was renowned for his iron will. But even this could not save his command from encirclement in the Ruhr pocket during March–April 1945. To avoid being only the second German or Prussian field marshal in history to be captured alive – after Paulus had met this ignominious fate at Stalingrad – Model committed suicide in mid-April after first disbanding his doomed command. (AKG Berlin)

the German Ruhr industrial zone. The Ninth US Army – now returned to Bradley's control – advanced from the Wesel bridgehead along the Ruhr's northern boundary, while the First US Army thrust south of the Ruhr from the Remagen bridgehead. Despite appalling odds, Army Group B commander Model remained determined to fulfil Hitler's orders to stand firm in the Ruhr. This region still delivered two-thirds of Germany's total industrial production, despite the vast damage done by Allied strategic bombing and Germany's belated attempts to decentralize its industrial base.

As the two American armies facing him pushed east, Model guessed that his cautious enemy would swing inward to clear the Ruhr before driving deeper into the Reich. Consequently, he organized his depleted regular ground forces – now reinforced with Home Guard units and Luftwaffe flak troops – to fight a protracted urban battle for the Ruhr that would inflict the horrific German experience of Stalingrad onto the Americans. The latter recognized the likely heavy costs involved in such an attritional struggle in the ruins of the Ruhr's cities, and instead sought to encircle the region in a deep pocket. On March 29, however, Model discerned Bradley's intent, and in desperation flung whatever meager reserves he possessed in a local riposte at Paderborn. Despite fanatical resistance, these scratch forces failed to stop the First and Ninth US Armies linking up at Lippstadt on April 1, 1945 to encircle 350,000 troops in the Ruhr – a larger force than that trapped at Stalingrad.

Hitler forbade Model from breaking out and promised a miracle relief operation mounted by the Eleventh and Twelfth Armies, then being raised from Germany's last part-trained recruits as, in sheer desperation, the Germans closed their remaining training schools and flung these troops into the fray. Model, however, remained unimpressed by such Hitlerian fantasies, and so on April 15 – to avoid being the second German field marshal in history to be captured alive (after Paulus at Stalingrad) – Model dissolved his army group and committed suicide. By April 18, when German resistance in the Ruhr ended, 316,000 troops had entered captivity. The Western Allies had torn a hole right through the center of the Western Front, while to north and south, the *Westheer* was now rapidly disintegrating.

Hitler reacted to the catastrophic setbacks recently suffered on all fronts, as well as to growing signs of defeatism, by increasing the already draconian discipline under which German soldiers toiled. On April 2, for example, Hitler ordered the summary execution of any soldier who displayed defeatism by advocating surrender or retreat. Even Commander-in-Chief West Kesselring now reminded his soldiers that it was a German soldier's duty to die well. Although these strictures did foster continuing resistance, the main motivation behind such efforts remained the intense professionalism displayed by many German troops – qualities that kept front-line units cohesive despite appalling battlefield losses. Yet now Hitler again displayed his contempt for the army's professional officer corps by placing control of the Home Guard's defense of German cities in the hands of Nazi Party officials, despite the latter's lack of military experience.

In desperation, Hitler committed Germany to a popular "total war" against the Allies by exhorting the entire population to wage a "Werewolf" guerrilla struggle in enemy-occupied German territory. Despite extensive propaganda, in reality only a few hundred well-trained Nazi fanatics undertook Werewolf operations, which not surprisingly achieved little. Nazi propaganda also sought to boost German defensive resilience by publicizing the establishment

of a strong defensive position – termed the "National Redoubt" by the Allies – in the mountains of southeastern Bavaria and western Austria. In reality, this fortified region existed only on paper and when on April 22 Hitler decided to remain in Berlin to face his fate, any inclination to defend this mythical fortress ebbed away. Thankfully for the Allies, there would be no protracted fanatical Nazi last stand in the mountains, although Allied concern over such a prospect led them to attempt a swift advance through southwestern Germany.

Meanwhile, Patton's Third US Army had broken out of its Rhine bridgeheads during March 24–26 and, in the face of disorganized resistance, had fanned out in rapid thrusts to the northeast, east, and southeast. By May 4, Patton's forces had pushed 172 miles (275 km) across central Germany to capture Chemnitz and Bayreuth. Farther south, Patch's Seventh US Army crossed the Rhine at Mannheim and advanced southeast to seize Stuttgart, then Ulm on the Danube River, and finally Nuremberg on April 19. Simultaneously, the First French Army thrust across the Rhine at Strasbourg and advanced southeast toward Lake Constance. The objective of Patch's and de Lattre's armies was to capture the "National Redoubt" swiftly before the enemy could consolidate its strength in this region.

Between April 9 and May 2, the Second (British) Army continued its rapid advance through northern Germany. On April 15, it liberated the Belsen concentration camp and discovered – as the Americans would do later at Dachau – the heinous crimes that Hitler's regime had committed. Meanwhile, by April 19, the First Canadian Army had liberated all of northeastern Holland and cut off the remaining German forces in northwestern Holland. The German forces caught in this strategically worthless pocket continued to resist until VE-Day, but largely because the Allies only masked the region and instead focused on more important operations in Germany. Subsequently, during April 19–27, Dempsey's three corps reached the Elbe River and then – with reinforcements

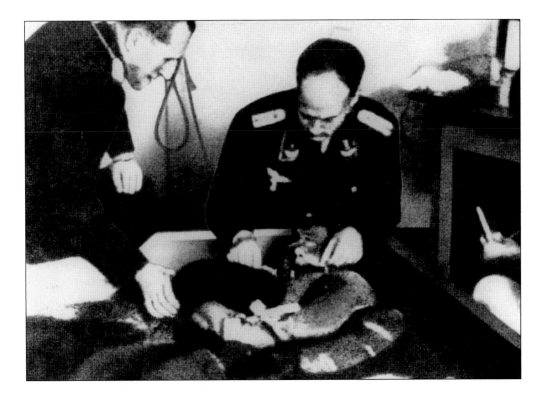

As the Western Allies advanced through the heart of the Reich, the full horrors committed by Hitler's regime became apparent. At Dachau inmates were used as human guinea pigs in experiments conducted by the Nazis. Here, a man is subjected to freezing experiments. (Topham Picturepoint)

from XVIII US Airborne Corps – dashed northeast against light opposition to reach the Baltic Sea at Wismar on May 2, thus securing Denmark's southern borders just hours before the Red Army arrived.

In the Allied center during April 2–19, Bradley's divisions struck east, rapidly overrunning central Germany and reaching the Elbe near Magdeburg. Here Eisenhower ordered the Ninth US Army to stop and to wait for the westward Soviet advance to prevent any local confrontations with the Red Army. During the next week, Hodges' First US Army overcame the hedgehog defense mounted by the still-forming German Eleventh Army in the Harz mountains to reach its designated halt-line on the Elbe and Mulde rivers along a 160-mile (256 km) front. Although Hodges' army remained static on the Elbe–Mulde Line during late April, on the 25th an American patrol did push farther east to link up with the Red Army at Strehla near Torgau. Between them the Allies had split the Reich in two, an eventuality for which the Germans had prepared by creating a

northern and southern Armed Forces High Command headquarters.

In Bradley's southern sector, on April 29 Patton's reinforced Third US Army commenced the last major American offensive of the war, striking rapidly east and southeast to seize Pilsen in Czechoslovakia and Linz in Austria, respectively. By now the news of Hitler's death had filtered through to German soldiers, and this led many to surrender after only token resistance. Consequently, during May 4, Patton's forces secured Linz; but just as he prepared to unleash his armor for a dash to Prague, Eisenhower stopped him to avoid any clash with the Soviets.

Meanwhile, farther south, Patch's Seventh US Army thrust through the supposed Nazi "National Redoubt" against only light

resistance during late April. Then, on May 1, Patch's forces secured the Alpine passes of the Austrian Tyrol, before dashing through the Brenner Pass on May 4 to link up with the Fifth US Army in northern Italy. By then, German resistance had virtually collapsed everywhere except the Eastern Front, and several German commanders in the west – as well as Dönitz's new Nazi regime – had begun to discuss surrender terms with the Allies. The Northwest Europe campaign was now set to enter its final hours.

The final collapse of the Third Reich became imminent once American and Soviet forces linked up with each other at Strehla near Torgau in central Germany on April 25, 1945, thus cutting what remained of the German state in half. The desperate Germans had anticipated such a development, however, and had even created two military authorities – one for the north and one for the south – for the moment when the Allies bisected Germany. (AKG Berlin)

Donald Burgett

Sprinting low to the ground, his feet surrounded by bursts of machine-gun fire, Donald Burgett glanced over his shoulder to glimpse a German Tiger tank lurching toward him. It was December 19, 1944, in a field on the northeastern outskirts of Noville, near Bastogne in the Belgian Ardennes. Intense enemy fire had just set alight the haystack in which Burgett had sought cover, and now the raging flames forced him to dash across the open, snow-covered fields back toward the shelter of nearby houses – a dash that would expose him to deadly enemy fire.

Luckily making it unscathed to a nearby house, Burgett rushed into a room to find two of his squad buddies already hiding there. Looking back through the glassless window frame, however, the paratroopers saw the Tiger approaching the house, and so dashed out of the back door. Within seconds the tank had advanced so that its gun barrel actually pointed through what used to be the front window of the house: then it fired its lethal 88mm cannon. Burgett scarcely avoided the tons of ruined brick that came crashing down on his nearby hiding place as the building's back wall disintegrated. He had survived this close shave, he mused, but for how long could he avoid that lethal enemy bullet "that had his name marked on it"?

By now a campaign veteran – he had dropped from the skies on D-Day – Burgett realized that the battle at Noville had been his most terrifying combat experience to date. But luckily for historians, Burgett not only survived the campaign, but also wrote down his recollections not long after VE-Day and then published them in a poignant memoir, *Seven Roads to Hell*, during the 1990s.

During the campaign, Burgett served as a private in the 2nd Platoon, A Company, 506th Parachute Infantry Regiment, part of the elite 101st US Airborne Division – the "Screaming Eagles." Born in Detroit, Michigan, in April 1926, he volunteered for the paratroopers in April 1943, on the day of his eighteenth birthday, having been previously turned down for being too young. On the night of June 5–6, 1944, he dropped with the rest of the "Screaming Eagles" behind German lines in the Cotentin peninsula to aid the imminent American D-Day landings on "Utah" beach. On June 13 he was wounded twice in bitter fighting near Carentan, first by a grenade detonation that left him temporarily deaf, and then by a shell fragment that tore open his left side. After three weeks in hospital, he returned to his division, which soon came out of the front line for much-needed replenishment.

Burgett then dropped with his division around Zon in Holland on September 17, 1944, as part of Montgomery's ambitious Market-Garden offensive. After fighting its way north through Nijmegen, Burgett's company held the front near Arnhem for nine weeks of mostly static actions amid sodden low-lying terrain. Eventually, on November 28, after 72 days' continuous action, the "Screaming Eagles" redeployed to northern France for rest and recuperation.

On December 17, 1944, as news filtered through about the success achieved by the surprise German Ardennes counteroffensive, Burgett's division rushed north to help defend the vital road junction at Bastogne. During December 19–20, Burgett's company resolutely defended Noville against the determined attacks launched by the 2nd Panzer Division. The next day, the Germans outflanked the 506th Regiment, forcing the Americans to conduct a costly withdrawal south through the village of Foy. Over the next week, however, in a series of bitter engagements, Burgett's company

The town of Bastogne represented the key communications node that
General Hasso von Manteuffel's Fifth Panzer Army had to capture so that
it could open up the southern axis of advance in the Battle of the Bulge.
The determined resistance offered by the 101st US Airborne Division
around Bastogne – as demonstrated at Noville during December 19–20 –
ensured that the encircled town never fell into German hands. (US Army)

At Marvie, a village located just to the east of Bastogne, fierce
resistance by American paratroopers helped prevent German
armor from dashing into Bastogne before a defensive perimeter
could be consolidated. When the Germans invited the
surrounded American garrison to surrender, the reply of their
commander was terse: "Nuts!" (US Army)

helped drive the Germans back to the start lines they had held prior to the commencement of their counterstrike.

Burgett's recollections vividly captured the brutal realities of combat in the Northwest Europe campaign – the diseases that afflicted soldiers, the terrible wounds suffered in battle, the awful food on which they had to subsist, and the intense emotions generated by these experiences. For example, he recalled with horror the diseases that lengthy exposure to Holland's wet conditions caused among the front-line troops. Burgett himself suffered from trench mouth, an ailment that made his gums ooze with pus and left his teeth so loose that he could easily move them with his tongue. Although penicillin eventually cured him, he then succumbed to trench foot after his boots disintegrated due to the length of his continuous front-line service in sodden terrain.

Scabies was another problem from which Burgett's company suffered in Holland, an unpleasant condition where microscopic parasites develop under the skin, causing insatiable itching. Such a disease flourished in the unhygienic conditions in which the paratroopers often served. Indeed, while in the front line near Arnhem, Burgett's comrades only occasionally managed to take what they termed a ". . . Bath" – a quick scrub of the head, armpits and crotch with icy cold water collected in their helmets. It was only when the division went on leave in France during late October 1944 that Burgett managed to take his first hot shower in 10 weeks!

Sanitary arrangements, too, were often rudimentary. During the 101st Division's dash north to Bastogne on a bitterly cold December 17, for example, the 380 open-topped cattle trucks that carried the paratroopers did not stop at all during the 24-hour journey, not even for a quick toilet stop. This meant that those unfortunate soldiers who could not wait any longer had to perform their bodily functions over the back of the truck's tail gate.

Such lack of hygiene, of course, proved a particularly serious problem for those paratroopers unlucky enough to be wounded in battle. Burgett recalled the moment during the savage December 19 battle for Noville when a new replacement soldier suddenly ran into view around the corner of a building, screaming in agony. Enemy fire had caught him in the stomach, and in his arms he carried most of his intestines, the remainder dragging along the ground through the dirt.

It took Burgett and two of his squad to hold down the sobbing soldier so that they could carry out emergency first aid. Laying a tattered raincoat down on the ground, the paratroopers placed the injured man on it and proceeded to wash his entrails, picking out the larger bits of dirt as best they could, before shoving his guts back inside his wide-open abdomen. They then tore the raincoat into strips, bound the man's midriff with this filthy makeshift bandage, and gave him the vital shot of morphine that each soldier carried. Finally, they dragged the wounded private into the relative safety of a nearby ditch while another trooper dashed off in search of a medic – all this being undertaken while enemy artillery rained down on their location. While such desperate measures undoubtedly saved many wounded soldiers' lives, the filthy conditions in which the wounds were either inflicted or initially treated often subsequently led soldiers to succumb to virulent infections.

Apart from the ever-present fear of death or serious injury, the other concern that dominated the paratroopers' lives, Burgett recalled, was food. A soldier's aluminum mess kit – bowl, knife, and fork – was his most important possession next to his weapon. If a soldier lost his mess kit in action, there were seldom any replacements, and the luckless individual had to use his helmet to take his ration from the regimental field kitchen. In tactical situations that allowed soldiers to draw food from the field kitchen, Burgett would always sprint to the front of the queue, then wolf down his food – just on the off-chance that if he rushed to the back of the queue, there might just be enough left over for some meager seconds.

For much of the time at the front, however, the fighting prevented hot food from reaching the troops, and then the soldiers had to subsist on boiling up their dehydrated K-Rations and "consuming" their D-Bars. The unpopular K-Rations were stodgy, lumpy, and tasteless substances but – as Burgett recollected – if you had not eaten for several days, even K-Rations could taste tolerable. Even more unpopular, however, was the D-Bar, a moldy-tasting so-called chocolate bar. These were so hard, Burgett maintained, that you could not smash one with your rifle butt, or melt it by boiling! Burgett insisted that he never successfully managed to consume a single bar throughout the campaign.

Apart from fear, disease, discomfort, and hunger, many of the other emotions that Burgett experienced during the campaign stayed with him. He vividly remembered, for instance, the odd little superstitions that some soldiers held. Many paratroopers from America's southern states would never take the first sip out of a liquid container that had a closed lid: as you opened the lid, so the old-wives' tale went, the Devil lurking inside would get you. Burgett also recollected that when a veteran "Old Sweat" experienced a premonition of his own impending death, very often that individual would be killed by enemy fire in the following days.

Although Burgett himself did not experience any such frightening premonitions, he was well acquainted with the phenomenon of abject terror. He recalled, for example, the sense of mind-numbing fear that overwhelmed him during one phase of the battle for Noville. He lay, heart pounding and sick with nausea, in the bottom of a slit trench just outside the town, while German Panther tanks moved round the American positions, systematically spraying the frozen ground with their machine guns. With no bazookas or satchel charges available, Burgett and his comrades had no choice but to press their bodies into the mud at the bottom of their trenches and pray that the tanks did not come close enough to collapse the trench on top of

them. The fear of a horrible death by crushing or suffocation effectively paralyzed him and left him almost unable to breathe. Burgett even remembered that at one point the enemy tanks were so close that he could feel the heat of their engines warming the bitter winter's air.

Perhaps surprisingly, even when the enemy came as close to Burgett as they had at Noville, he merely regarded them as abstract objects – either you killed them first, or else they killed you. Rarely did the enemy individuals whom he faced in close-quarter combat register as human beings in his mind for more than a few hours. Usually, the immediate requirements of staying alive and accomplishing the mission took priority over any sense of compassion for his opponents.

One particular German soldier, however, stayed in Burgett's mind long after the war had ended. The incident occurred in late December 1944, as the paratroopers drove the Germans back to the positions that they had held before the Ardennes counteroffensive commenced. In a dense wood, Burgett came across a wounded, and obviously helpless, enemy soldier. As Burgett contemplated what to do, one of his comrades stepped up and shot the German dead. Burgett exploded in anger, grabbed his comrade, and threatened to blow his brains out if he ever again shot a German who was attempting to surrender. For the rest of the campaign, in quiet moments between engagements, the imploring face of this anonymous enemy soldier would return to haunt Burgett's thoughts.

Few sources reveal the often-unpleasant realities that ordinary soldiers faced in war better than a soldier's memoirs written close to the events. This certainly remains true of Donald Burgett's recollections. Whether it be the strange superstitions, the unpleasant rations, or the heroism of emergency first aid dispensed to a wounded comrade while under enemy fire, any study of the Northwest Europe campaign is enriched by drawing on such vivid memories of those individuals who participated in its events.

Rationing and retaliation

The Northwest Europe campaign exerted an influence on the nations involved in these operations that extended far beyond the battlefield. It impacted on both the international and domestic politics of the states prosecuting the campaign, as well as influencing powerfully their economies, societal fabrics, ethical attitudes, and cultural heritage. First, Anglo-American cooperation during the campaign cemented the transatlantic alliance between them and ensured that their "special relationship" flourished during the postwar period. In addition, the military necessity that underpinned the campaign dramatically increased cross-cultural interaction between the two nations, yet simultaneously generated cultural friction.

Inevitably, a proportion of the large numbers of American personnel stationed in the United Kingdom during 1943–45 formed relationships with British women; consequently, some British women became "GI Brides," and a generation of children were born to Anglo-American parents. The presence of American troops created friction with their male British counterparts because of their complaints about warm British beer, because of the luxuries they enjoyed, which few "Brits" had seen for years, and because of their success in attracting attention from British women. Underpinning this friction were mutual cultural ignorance, misunderstanding, and prejudice on the part of both peoples.

One area where this necessity of military cooperation exposed divergent cultural perspectives was the issue of race. The

American armed forces remained segregated into "white" and "colored" units and naturally they sought to continue this

In Central Germany on May 8, 1945 – Victory in Europe Day (VE-Day) – American soldiers met up with troops from the Red Army to celebrate their defeat of Hitler's heinous Nazi German Reich. (AKG Berlin)

segregation when deployed overseas in the United Kingdom and on the continent of Europe. But this attempt to export American racial segregation to the United Kingdom encountered considerable opposition from the British government and people, whose sense of fairness and solidarity with anyone fighting Nazi oppression, irrespective of their nationality, creed, or religion, was offended by such overt discrimination.

While the war strengthened ties between Britain and America, it accelerated the loosening of the bonds of the British Empire, including the Dominions as well as Britain's colonies. The Canadians, for example, were determined, for reasons of national pride, to retain the autonomy of the First Canadian Army throughout the Northwest Europe campaign; in contrast, the British War Office adopted a rather condescending attitude that

sought to keep Canadian troops under overall British military control. This tension dominated the professional relationship of Montgomery and Canadian General Henry Crerar during the 1944–45 campaign.

Thus operations in this theater tended to aggravate the already growing Canadian perception that their British "masters" could not avoid displaying an oppressive, imperialistic paternalism toward them. In the postwar era, this development increased the mounting domestic Canadian sentiment for full independence, a process that culminated in the 1982 Constitution Act's removal of the last vestiges of British authority over Canada.

The Northwest Europe campaign also changed domestic politics among the combatants. Nazi Germany had long been a one-party totalitarian dictatorship, so the campaign in this sense had little impact on German domestic politics. Yet the setbacks that the Wehrmacht experienced in Normandy did embolden the anti-Hitler resistance movement. This fostered the attempt to assassinate Adolf Hitler with a bomb positioned at the Führer's headquarters at Rastenburg in East Prussia on July 20, 1944, an attack that only narrowly failed. The Nazi state responded viciously to this attempted assassination, arresting, torturing, and executing in particularly gruesome ways the leading conspirators.

On the Allied side, Britain had formed a government of national unity early in the war and domestic partisan politics were largely, though not totally, subordinated to the greater needs of the war effort. In contrast, within the United States, domestic politics continued as usual. The Republicans, always more isolationist in outlook, used the war to mount partisan attacks against President Roosevelt's Democratic presidency and his continuation of New Deal policies.

The campaign exerted a more marked impact on Canadian domestic politics. The need to provide more manpower for the theater provoked a domestic political crisis in Canada during 1944. In the first phase of the war, the Canadian government could only send volunteers to serve overseas. Then, in 1942 the Canadian people passed a referendum allowing the government to dispatch overseas conscripts called up under the National Resources Mobilization Act (NRMA) of 1941. Unfortunately, francophone Quebec continued its traditional hostility toward the pro-British Canadian government and voted overwhelmingly against the referendum.

Fearful of exercising the authority conferred upon it by the people, the Canadian government prevaricated and refrained from dispatching conscripts to northwest Europe long after they were desperately needed. The Prime Minister, Mackenzie King, hoped that the war would end before he would have to exercise such controversial authority. But the heavy Canadian casualties suffered at Falaise, as well as in clearing the Channel ports and the Scheldt, left the Canadians significantly deficient in combat troops.

Reluctantly, therefore, in November 1944 the Canadian government decided to send the "Zombies" (as Canada's volunteer soldiers derisively dubbed the conscripts) to northwest Europe. They arrived tardily and in the face of considerable opposition both domestically and from the "Zombies" themselves. In fact, extremely serious absence without leave and desertion problems emerged among the "Zombies" soon after they arrived in northwest Europe and few saw extensive combat service.

Economically, World War II brought material deprivation for the civilians of all the protagonists. The Northwest Europe campaign was no exception. Every nation resorted to varying degrees of rationing, although the United States, protected by its geographic isolation from the war in Europe, was the least affected by domestic food rationing. Britain, with its maritime lines of communication threatened by U-boat attacks, introduced stringent rationing early and launched a major campaign for self-sufficiency, which produced the allotments that can still occasionally be found even today in British cities and towns.

In the case of Germany, Hitler at first kept rationing to an absolute minimum in order to protect the civilian morale that had collapsed in the latter stages of the Great War. But as the war turned against Germany and defeats in the west added to those in the east and south, rationing became progressively more stringent. Rationing was

One of the chief privations suffered by the British people during World War II was stringent rationing of food and goods through the use of the coupon system. With German U-boats attempting to strangle the supply of foodstuffs and manufactured goods arriving into Britain from across the seas, the British government also had to embark on a crusade for agricultural self-sufficiency and manufacturing. The former was made possible by the creation of thousands of small allotments in urban areas. (ISI)

also extensive for French, Belgian, and Dutch civilians until released from German occupation by the Allied advance across northwest Europe. Since the Germans ruthlessly stripped France of resources and productive capacity to support the German war effort, civilians were forced to make do on meager rations.

Subsistence was particularly difficult for the Dutch population cut off in the isolated "Fortress Netherlands," in the north of the country, during spring 1945. The Germans had extensively flooded the low-lying land to hamper the Allied advance, but this measure also drowned large areas of farmland. The combination of flooded land, the general wartime dislocation of agricultural and economic production, and large-scale German depredations ensured that in spring 1945 the occupied Netherlands was unable to meet its basic subsistence needs and thus the populace slowly began to starve to death. Indeed, ration quotas sank so low that, in desperation, the German command was forced to allow the Allies to fly in foodstuffs for the civilian population during the last weeks of the war.

Societies in transition

Socially, World War II, like all total wars, provided a motor for accelerated social change and a general relaxation of social mores among all the combatants. The departure of so many men to war, the massive relocation of individuals from self-contained rural environments to cities, and the ever-present prospect of death threatened the sanctity of marriage, and saw an explosion of premarital sex and casual sexual encounters. Indeed, the experiences of the war dramatically increased the acceptability of casual sex, and while postwar governments and societies tried hard to restore prewar social values, they were never entirely successful. For soldiers away from wives and sweethearts, military service exposed them to the temptations of

prostitutes, and thus introduced the dangers of venereal diseases.

The four years of German occupation inevitably brought extensive "fraternization" between French, Belgian, and Dutch women and German soldiers as well. One of the saddest aspects of the Allied liberation of France was the social ostracism and violence directed by both the Resistance (Maquis) and ordinary French civilians against women who had "fraternized" with the enemy: many of these individuals suffered physical abuse, forcible shaving of their heads, and public humiliation. In fact, the Allied liberation brought a more general vicious settling of scores against alleged collaborators. In the Channel Islands – the only part of the British Isles to fall under Nazi occupation – the issue of collaboration continued to divide this once tightly knit community for several decades after 1945.

These retaliations reflected one particular unfortunate effect of total war on the populations involved: that the experience of violence begets more violence. This, as de Gaulle's regime found in France during 1945, made it difficult to return swiftly to prewar civilian control following the liberation from Nazi occupation.

The war also gave British, American, and Canadian women, at least, dramatically increased opportunities for participation in the war effort. Women served extensively in the defense industries, freeing men for combat duty. They served as auxiliaries at headquarters, in communications, as well as in administrative and medical services. Here they not only made invaluable contributions to the Allied victory, but lived very different lives from those they would have experienced if the war had not erupted. Young women enjoyed much greater independence, paying their own way,

Right. Once the Allies had liberated parts of Nazi-occupied northwest Europe, alleged collaborators found themselves facing harsh summary "justice." French women – such as this individual – who had collaborated with the Germans had their hair shaved off and were treated as social outcasts. (AKG Berlin)

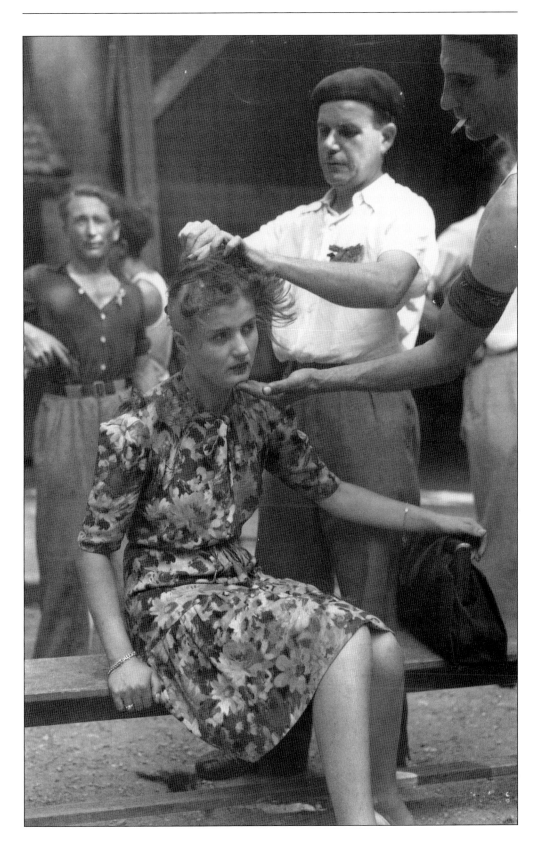

Like most "total wars," the harsh demands placed on the state during the 1939–45 war by its need to prosecute the conflict led to rapid social change. British women, for example, worked extensively in the war economy, as well as undertaking auxiliary functions within the armed and public forces, such as manning antiaircraft defenses and fighting fires. (ISI)

working away from family, and being surrounded by like-minded friends.

In contrast, Hitler refused to mobilize women more extensively for the German war effort, and this represented one of Germany's greatest strategic mistakes of the war. Reflecting the traditional, patriarchal gender roles that National Socialism extolled, Hitler saw the principal wartime role of women as simply to produce and nurture a new generation of blond-haired, blue-eyed Aryan Nazi warriors. The Nazi failure to harness its female population more extensively to support the war effort, as did their Allied opponents, contributed directly to the defeat of Nazi Germany in May 1945.

World War II was truly a "total" war. One manifestation of this was the unprecedented mobilization of youth for war. This was particularly true of totalitarian Germany. As the tide of war turned against them, the Germans progressively accepted younger and younger volunteers into the military. These volunteers, who underwent preliminary premilitary training, were drawn from the paramilitary Hitler Youth movement.

In 1943, for example, the Nazis raised the 12th SS Panzer Division Hitler Youth, consisting of 17–18-year-old volunteers, and the division distinguished itself repeatedly during the northwest Europe campaign. So young were these soldiers that they were not allowed the standard armed forces cigarette ration, instead receiving boiled sweets! Despite their youth, or perhaps because of it, they proved some of the most fanatical Nazi soldiers, having endured years of intensive ideological indoctrination and propaganda. This fanaticism manifested itself in the fields of Normandy in war crimes, in which Hitler Youth Division soldiers murdered Canadian troops who had surrendered.

Combatant or civilian?

Another dimension of both World War II and the 1944–45 campaign as total conflicts was the increasing blurring of the distinction between civilians and combatants, and the resultant increasing "collateral" damage suffered by civilian populations. This was particularly true of the air war. Buoyed by the strategic bombing theorists' misguided mantra that air power could single-handedly win the war by

destroying the morale of the German civilian population, the Western Allies launched massed attacks by heavy bombers on German industrial and urban targets.

While RAF Bomber Command attacked German cities at night, the United States Army Air Force pursued daylight precision attacks against centers of German industry. The result was the deaths of hundreds of thousands of German civilians and the diversion of massive German resources into passive and active countermeasures,

including static antiaircraft artillery batteries, searchlights, early warning radar, bomb shelters, and rescue services, as well as day and night fighters.

For German civilians the last two years of the war were a story of increasing terror as Allied aircraft launched attacks of increasing intensity and lethality. They culminated in the Dresden bombing of February 1945, where casualties were not that far below those suffered in the subsequent atomic bomb drops on

During 1944–45, as Germany's battlefield situation deteriorated further, an increasingly desperate regime began to draft younger and younger Hitler Youth teenagers into the armed services to replace the vast casualties suffered on all three fronts. The German Home Guard Militia (*Volkssturm*) comprised young boys, pensioners, the infirm, and essential war workers previously exempted from military service. (ISI)

Hiroshima and Nagasaki. For the Allied air crews carrying out these missions, their task proved to be one of the most dangerous military occupations of World War II. Despite the prewar claims that the bombers "would always get through," often they did not, and thousands were shot down

and their crews killed, maimed, or taken prisoner.

During spring 1944 the Allies turned their fleets of heavy bombers toward France and began an interdiction campaign intended to isolate the Normandy invasion site. The Allies bombed bridges, railway stations, and marshalling yards, particularly along the Seine and Loire rivers. So intensive were these attacks that by D-Day the Allies had destroyed every major rail bridge into Normandy and the Loire and Seine rivers, isolating the Normandy battlefield. At the same time, however, so as not to give away

The prolonged Allied strategic bombing campaign against Germany inflicted appalling damage on buildings and caused heavy civilian casualties. Despite this, the campaign failed – in contradiction to the ideas of the interwar theorists – to break the will of Germany's populace to continue the war. (IWM B7754)

the invasion site, the Allied bombers had to deliberately dissipate their attacks to disguise the location of the actual invasion, striking targets of opportunity all across northern and western France.

While this bombing campaign did achieve its aim of crippling France's communications and hampering German redeployment and movement, unfortunately it also inflicted thousands of casualties on French civilians. This was particularly true of the novel carpet-bombing attacks, in which heavy bombers were used in direct support of ground forces on the battlefield. First tried at Monte Cassino in Italy during spring 1944, this was a very complex and inherently hazardous

application of air power. It required great precision, depended heavily on technology for its accuracy, yet was subject to human error. It therefore had mixed success. One of the most tragic incidents of unintended "collateral damage" was the July 7, 1944, raid on Caen, which killed more than 700 French civilians and flattened much of the medieval part of the town. The raid barely scratched the German defenders deployed on the city's northern perimeter.

Another new feature of World War II was the development of rockets capable of hitting both military and civilian targets over long distances. The Germans responded to the Allied D-Day landings in Normandy by initiating their V1 "Vengeance" rocket attacks on London, beginning on June 10, 1944. Because the V1 lacked accuracy and Hitler thirsted to avenge the Allied strategic bombing campaign, the Führer launched these rockets at the civilian population of southern England. These "Buzz Bombs," as the British dubbed them, proved difficult to intercept and shoot down, and could rain indiscriminate havoc down on British towns.

However, such attacks failed to break British civilian morale – just as the German bombing "Blitz" of 1940 had failed to do. In fact, deploying the V1 represented an unproductive diversion of precious Nazi resources. Though they did require considerable Allied resources to counter them, they were wrongly targeted at civilians. Instead, Hitler should have employed them against the Allied invasion fleet and Normandy bridgehead, where they could have hampered and disrupted Allied military operations.

The supersonic, jet-propelled V2 missile that the Germans unleashed during autumn 1944 proved more damaging. The Germans employed this deadlier missile to better effect, directing many of their strikes against the crucial port of Antwerp, through which flowed the bulk of Allied supplies for the entire northwest Europe theater. For the Belgian citizens of Antwerp this was a terrifying manifestation of total war that was very difficult to stop, and it caused considerable civilian loss of life.

Another situation in which innocent civilians became unwitting victims of war in northwest Europe was the reprisal policy that the Germans implemented in retaliation for sabotage and assassination attacks by the Resistance. The German occupying forces frequently executed 10 civilians for every German soldier killed or wounded in such strikes. The most egregious massacres occurred after D-Day as heightened levels of Maquis attacks threatened the German lines of communication within rural France.

The worst German reprisal atrocity occurred at Oradour-sur-Glane on June 10. Here, troops of the 2nd SS Panzer Division *Das Reich*, in addition to carrying out many summary executions, herded the bulk of the village's population into the church and set it alight. In total, the Germans murdered 642 innocent French civilians in reprisal for the death of just one of its officers in a Maquis ambush.

Similarly, thousands of French Resistance fighters captured by the Germans both prior to and during the northwest Europe campaign were tortured and executed by the occupiers, including the famous French social historian Marc Bloch. In addition, as the prospect of liberation loomed large, Allied forces having established themselves in Normandy after D-Day, a particularly vicious cycle of assassination and reprisal emerged between the Maquis and pro-Nazi French collaborationist paramilitary organizations such as the *Milice*.

The Nazi Holocaust

The Germans compelled thousands of French, Belgian, and Dutch men to "volunteer" for labor service within the Reich, where they were poorly treated, overworked, and subject to high fatality and injury rates through industrial accidents. The Germans, of course, also deported "racial and political" enemies to both forced labor and concentration camps. During their occupation of France, the Germans, aided by French anti-Semites, rounded up and deported the bulk of the country's prewar Jewish population. Most of France's Jews – some 77,300 individuals – met a grisly death in Nazi concentration and extermination camps, together with 129,000 Dutch and Belgian Jews. Those who tried to shelter deportees also risked deportation or execution themselves.

In fact, the Nazi "New Order" in France encouraged the latent racism and anti-Semitism ingrained in sections of western society to flourish anew. In France, the Netherlands, and Belgium, pro-fascist parties and movements often eagerly cooperated with the Nazis in identifying, rounding up, and deporting Jews and other racial enemies of the Reich. Such political organizations hoped to be allowed to govern their home countries under benevolent Nazi stewardship once Germany had won the war. The latter's defeat in 1945 probably obscured the fact that the Nazis had little inclination

The railway spur inside Birkenau, looking back toward the main gate. Birkenau was the labor camp attached to Auschwitz, the most infamous of the Nazi extermination camps, where Hitler's minions enacted their heinous "Final Solution of the Jewish problem" – the extermination of 5.5 million of Europe's Jews. (AKG Berlin)

to permit the sort of autonomy aspired to by these local fascist parties.

Censorship was widely enacted by all the combatants during World War II In Nazi Germany and its occupied territories it was near total. One important resistance activity was to publish clandestine "free" presses, while millions of people in German-occupied Europe daily risked arrest and deportation to listen on the radio to the BBC Overseas Service for developments in the war. Even among the Western Allied powers fighting to free occupied Europe from Nazi oppression, wartime necessity compelled the suspension of many normal civil rights. Under the slogan "careless talk cost lives," extensive restrictions were placed on the freedom of the press.

Such restrictions reached their height during the preparations for Operation Overlord, the D-Day landings. Those few privileged individuals in the know as to the date and location of the invasion were allocated an extra top-secret security clearance designated "Bigot." Pre-invasion paranoia led to some unfortunate detentions.

One individual was arrested for publicly calling another man, who by coincidence possessed a "Bigot" security clearance, a bigot. Though he was talking about the individual's narrowed-minded, prejudiced views, fears of a security leak led to his arrest! Another unfortunate victim was a national crossword designer who inadvertently included a number of the code names for the D-Day landing beaches in a crossword. For fear that he was a Nazi spy communicating clandestinely with his bosses, he was arrested and detained until after the invasion had taken place.

The 1944–45 campaign, as well as the wider World War II, did considerable damage to European culture. The Nazis, no lovers of diversity anyway, seized enormous quantities of artwork and forms of cultural expression from the states of northwest Europe; many of these pieces were never seen again after 1945 and of those that did emerge, only a small proportion were ever returned to their rightful owners. With their narrow, traditional artistic tastes, the Nazis labeled many manifestations of the avant-garde, progressive art that flourished during the anxiety-laden interwar era as "degenerate." This, of course, included any expressions of Jewish, Gypsy (Roma), or African-American culture and heritage.

Western architecture suffered significant damage due to both the extensive ground operations conducted in northwest Europe during 1944–45 and the protracted Allied strategic bombing campaign. Some of the most famous architectural monuments of western Europe, including the German cathedrals of Cologne and Aachen, as well as Notre Dame in Paris and St. Paul's in London, all suffered varying degrees of damage that necessitated extensive postwar reconstruction.

The gravest cultural damage inflicted during World War II, however, was the Holocaust: the Nazis' genocide against the Jews of Europe. In what constituted one of the worst crimes committed in history,

Hitler's regime came perilously close to successfully eradicating Jewish culture in Europe. Only the combined success of the Western Allied campaigns in northwest Europe and Italy, and the Soviet advance from the east, ensured that Hitler's Reich was defeated in May 1945 before this heinous mission was completed.

Many of Europe's most impressive architectural sites suffered extensive damage during the 1939–45 war, due either to ground fighting or to aerial bombing. This image depicts St. Paul's Cathedral surrounded by fires after a Luftwaffe bombing attack on London during the "Blitz" of 1940. (Ann Ronan Picture Library)

Brenda McBryde

The campaign proved just as crucial an experience for the noncombatants involved in the theater as for those soldiers who served in the front line. One such noncombatant was nurse Brenda McBryde, who was born just 10 days before the armistice ended World War I. During 1938, Brenda started a four-year course of nursing training at the Royal Victoria Infirmary, Newcastle upon Tyne. In April 1943 she qualified as a state registered nurse and then was commissioned into the British army as a nursing officer in the Queen Alexandra's Imperial Military Nursing Service (Reserve). After seven months' service with the 75th British General Hospital at Peebles in Scotland, Brenda moved with this unit to Sussex in preparation for commitment to France once the Western Allies' Second Front had commenced. Within a fortnight of D-Day, the 75th had redeployed to the village of Rys in Normandy, close to the coastal town of Arromanches.

During her nursing service in northwest Europe, Brenda encountered some grisly sights in the field hospital, but years of professional training helped her to take these experiences in her stride. The most depressing duty that Brenda faced, she recalled, was working in the head injuries ward. A large proportion of these soldiers had lapsed into comas, and these patients Brenda had to feed with milk, egg, and glucose inserted through a nasal tube. The biggest problems for such patients, Brenda recollected, was that their permanently half-open mouths would become infected during that summer's hot humid weather. In the absence of eating that produced saliva to cleanse the mouth, the coma victims' mouths soon became encrusted with pus, and so Brenda had to cleanse their gums with antiseptic many times each day. Sadly, only a few of the patients ever woke from their comas.

When deployed in Normandy, the 75th also treated injured enemy soldiers who had been captured. Brenda's experiences in treating enemy troops enabled her to form distinct – if stereotypical – impressions of the German soldier's character. Her hospital only received large numbers of enemy wounded during the rapid Allied advance of August 1944, forcing it to create entire wards just for enemy prisoners, and these wards soon took on national characteristics. The wounded Germans, Brenda noticed, soon became distressed by the lack of rules as to what was or was not permitted on the ward. Within an hour of the creation of the first exclusively German ward, the enemy patients had appointed a duty officer, whom Brenda derogatorily addressed as the "Tent-Meister." This individual would shout "Achtung!" every time a nurse entered the ward, and all the conscious patients, lying on their beds, would click their heels together in response. But the formidable hospital matron soon put a stop to this nonsense: "We'll have none of your nasty Nazi habits here," she said in her best commanding voice, as she brusquely turned over the nearest German patient and enthusiastically rammed a penicillin needle into the hapless individual's buttocks!

Brenda soon realized, however, that most of the wounded Germans, who increasingly were young lads and old men, were little different from her wounded Allied patients. Indeed, on one occasion, a moving incident occurred that shed much poignancy on the absurdity of war. One morning a young German began to sing the popular soldier's song "Lili Marlene," and when the nurses failed to hush him down, the rest of his convalescing comrades joined in. Next, from the adjacent ward, British patients began to sing the same song – in English instead of German – until an enthusiastic but good-natured competition developed between them. Brenda recalled that this display of spontaneous high spirits broke the gloom that continually hung over the wards.

Some German patients, however, proved to be very different from the rest of their comrades. On one occasion, for example, Brenda treated a barely conscious German trooper who had lost one leg; he was clearly identifiable as a member of the elite Waffen-SS by his silver and black collar runes. As she fed the patient a glass of water, the soldier came to his senses, opened his eyes and instinctively smiled at the individual who was tending to him. Within seconds, however, after his vision had focused on Brenda's uniform, his grateful demeanor suddenly changed. With a convulsive jerk, the SS-trooper spat into her face and screeched, with whatever venom he could muster, a string of obscenities at her. Brenda's commanding officer had witnessed the incident and in a voice hard with anger, he instructed the staff not to treat the SS soldier until all the other newly arrived cases had been dealt with. That was the only time in Normandy that Brenda recalled a German patient being treated differently from a British one: irrespective of nationality, patients were treated in strict order according to the severity of their injuries.

During her service in northwest Europe, Brenda also encountered the discomforts that even noncombatants had to face during wartime. For seven weeks in Normandy, for example, she went without a hot bath, making do with a quick rinse every morning and night with cold water carried in a large biscuit tin. Then, in early August, the nurses heard of a French convent near Bayeaux where you could get a hot bath for just a few francs. So one morning, when she had a rare spell of off-duty time not consumed with sleep induced by exhaustion, Brenda and two of her fellow nurses went on a bathing trip. They arranged a lift in a borrowed jeep, and arrived at the convent only to find a large queue at the entrance: obviously, good news traveled fast in times of adversity. Carrying – like everyone else in the queue – a rolled-up towel and a modest piece of soap, all three waited patiently in line for their turn. When they got to the head of

the queue, Brenda paid the sister a few francs and entered the tiny whitewashed hut. Inside, Brenda undressed and slipped into the deep copper bath, filled with steaming hot water. What bliss!

When all three nurses had finished this luxurious experience, they topped it with another treat that had been denied them for months – a drink at a coffeehouse. Admittedly, the "coffee" was just an ersatz brew made from ground acorns that tasted like stewed boots. But despite this, Brenda found that just being able to relax and view the world around her for a few minutes was in itself a luxury after an incessant seven-week cycle of tending patients, bolting down unappetizing food, sleeping, and then resuming her duties.

As Brenda worked in a field hospital deployed close to the front line, she also faced the hardship of limited availability of food. The only hot beverage available was "Compo Tea," an insipid drink made from a cube of dehydrated tea, milk and sugar. It was usually "brewed" in a large bucket and carried around the wards for staff and patients alike. The nurses often had to use biscuit tins to drink this unappetizing concoction due to a shortage of mugs. Food remained quite restricted, and this proved a problem for those patients who required a high-protein diet.

Brenda hit on the idea of trading with the local French population. The nurses held a 30-minute outpatients' clinic every morning to treat the local population's minor injuries; after treatment, the nurses in return went round with their tin helmets to collect eggs and other farm produce. When the hospital's commanding officer heard about this unofficial activity, he simply made sure he was on the other side of the camp every time the outpatients' clinic took place, so that he never publicly "discovered" this sensible yet unauthorized arrangement.

These hardships became noticeably more intense in mid-July, when Brenda's commanding officer sent her and a colleague on temporary duty to a field dressing station just behind the front line. This proved necessary because storms had delayed the evacuation of wounded personnel back to

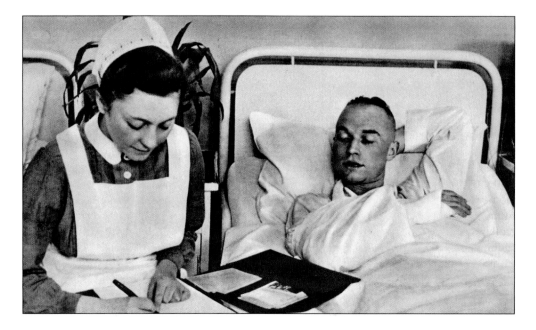

Britain and, consequently, a backlog of patients had emerged at their first point of call, the front-line dressing stations. As this was a combat zone, the conditions were rudimentary indeed. The nurses slept on camp beds in a 3ft-deep (1 m) trench that was roofed over with wooden planks and a canvas tent. Their latrine was simply a tent erected over a large pit in the ground. Every night, the exhausted nurses' sleep was disturbed by the ground-shaking effect of sustained artillery fire.

Understandably, the station commandant was concerned that the arrival of two nursing officers might have a marked impact on the platoon of engineers deployed to help construct its facilities. Consequently, he ordered that an official painted sign bearing the message, "Sisters' Quarters – Keep Out!" be erected outside the nurses' new "home." With typical soldiers' humor, within 24 hours a crudely painted sign had appeared outside the engineers' canvas-covered trenches, bearing the rejoinder, "Brothers' Quarters – Come In!"

Despite the commandant's efforts, the nurses nevertheless unwittingly caused quite a stir among the engineers. Once a week the nurses had their "bath night." They would stand under their tent – naked except for their tin hats – with each foot in a biscuit tin of cold water, and wash themselves down. It was only

Nurses working in field hospitals in both the UK and active combat theaters also faced some risk from enemy aerial bombing, in addition to the normal stresses associated with wartime nursing service. That said, the War Office believed that the presence of female nursing sisters in forward areas did provide a powerful boost to the morale of wounded soldiers. (AKG Berlin)

as they left the dressing station that one engineer confessed to them the interest that bath night had generated among the soldiers. The glare of the nurses' lamp meant that their illuminated silhouettes could be seen on the tent's canvas sides. After the word had got around, once a week the engineers would silently creep down toward the nurses' quarters to watch with fascination the latest performance of "bath night"!

These few incidents should make it clear that the campaign proved a pivotal experience for a young and, up to that point, relatively sheltered nurse such as Brenda McBryde. Noncombatants, as well as the front-line soldiers, clearly encountered real challenges in this campaign. Whether this was a distressing encounter with an ungrateful Nazi fanatic, or the touching experience of a spontaneous singing competition, or even the despair of treating coma patients with little chance of recovery, Brenda certainly saw a lot of life in her few months spent in northwest Europe.

The road to VE Day

The key event that made possible the end of the Northwest Europe campaign – and the entire World War II in Europe – occurred at 3:30 pm on April 30, 1945. At that moment, the German Führer, Adolf Hitler, committed suicide in the Reichschancellory Bunker in Berlin, as above ground triumphant Soviet forces advanced to within 330 yds (300 m) of this installation. Back on April 22, as Soviet spearheads began to encircle the German capital, Hitler had abandoned his notion of escaping to lead Germany's war from Berchtesgaden in Bavaria, and instead decided to remain in Berlin to meet his fate.

Even into the last hours of his life, Hitler remained determined that Germany would continue its desperate resistance against the Allied advance, if necessary to the last man and round, irrespective of the destruction that this would inflict on the German nation. With the Führer's death, so passed away this iron resolve to prosecute to the last a war that almost every German now recognized as already lost. On April 30, though, Hitler ordered that, once he had taken his own life, Grand Admiral Karl Dönitz, Commander-in-Chief of the Navy, should replace him as Führer. His successor, Hitler instructed, was to continue Germany's resistance to the Allies for as long as possible, irrespective of the cost.

A view of the entrance to the Reichschancellory Bunker near which Hitler's corpse was burned after his suicide on the afternoon of April 30, 1945. With his death, the Nazi leadership could now abandon Hitler's futile – and ultimately self-destructive – mantra of resistance to the last bullet. (AKG Berlin)

Yet even before the Führer's suicide, it seemed to him that several rats had already attempted to desert the sinking Nazi ship. On April 23, for example, Hitler's designated deputy, Reichsmarschall Hermann Göring, had informed Hitler – now surrounded in Berlin, but very much alive – that as the latter had lost his freedom of action, the Reichsmarschall would assume the office of Führer. An enraged Hitler, interpreting this as treason, relieved Göring of his offices and ordered his arrest.

The day before, Reichsführer-SS Heinrich Himmler had secretly met Count Folke Bernadotte of Sweden at Lübeck. At this meeting, Himmler offered to surrender all German armies facing the Western Allies, allowing the latter to advance east to prevent more German territory falling to the Soviets. The Reichsführer hoped that his offer would entice the Western Allies into continuing the war that Germany had waged since 1941 against the Soviet Union – the common enemy of all the states of Europe, Himmler believed. The Western Allies, however, remained committed to accept nothing other than Germany's simultaneous unconditional surrender to the

four major Allied powers. Moreover, they recognized Himmler's diplomatic approach as nothing more than a crude attempt to split their alliance with the Soviets, and so rejected Himmler's offer on April 27. When Hitler heard of Himmler's treachery on April 28, he ordered that his erstwhile "Loyal Heinrich" be arrested.

Simultaneously, and with Himmler's connivance, SS Colonel-General Karl Wolff, the German military governor of northern Italy, continued the secret negotiations that he had initiated with the Western Allies in February 1945 over the surrender of the German forces deployed in Italy. On April 29 – the day before Hitler's suicide – in another vain attempt to split the Allied alliance, a representative of General von Vietinghoff signed the instrument of surrender for the German forces located in Italy. By May 2,

During the period May 1–23, 1945, Admiral Karl Dönitz acted as Nazi Germany's Second Führer after Hitler's Last Testament named him as his successor. On May 23, however, the British arrested Dönitz and his cabinet at their Flensburg headquarters near the German–Danish border. Subsequently, Dönitz was tried by the Nuremberg Tribunal and sentenced to 10 years' imprisonment. (Imperial War Museum HU 3011)

some 300,000 German troops in this area had already laid down their arms.

On May 1, 1945, the new Führer, Karl Dönitz, established his headquarters at Flensburg near the German–Danish border in Schleswig-Holstein. Dönitz immediately abandoned Hitler's futile mantra of offering resistance to the last bullet, and accepted that the war was lost. Instead, Dönitz attempted merely to continue the war to save what could reasonably be rescued from the Soviets' grasp. By surrendering German forces piecemeal in the west, Dönitz hoped that the Western Allies would occupy most of the Reich to spare the bulk of the German nation from the horrors of Soviet occupation.

Furthermore, when the advancing Western Allies neared the rear lines of the German forces still locked in bitter resistance against the Soviets in the east, Dönitz hoped to withdraw these troops – plus the isolated garrisons of East Prussia and Courland – into Western Allied captivity. In this fashion, Dönitz hoped to save the bulk of the German army in the east from the nightmare of years of forced labor in Stalin's infamous prison camps.

But during May 1–2, 1945, Germany's already dire strategic situation deteriorated further, undermining Dönitz's strategy of calculated delaying actions. In that period, Montgomery's forces cut off Schleswig-Holstein from Germany by linking up with the Red Army on the Baltic coast, while the Americans consolidated their link-up with the Soviets in central Germany. Although on May 3 the German army could still field over five million troops, it was obvious to all that within a few days the Allies would overrun what little remained of Hitler's supposed Thousand-Year Reich.

Given these harsh realities, on the morning of Thursday May 3, Dönitz sent a delegation under a flag of truce to Montgomery's new tactical headquarters on the windswept Lüneberg Heath. The delegation wished to negotiate the surrender to Montgomery of not just the German forces that faced the 21st Army Group but

also the three German armies of Army Group Vistula then resisting the Soviets in Mecklenburg and Brandenburg.

Montgomery stated that he would accept the surrender of all German forces that faced him in northwestern Germany and Denmark, but could not accept that of those facing the Red Army, who had to surrender to the Soviets. If the Germans did not immediately surrender, Montgomery brutally warned, his forces would continue their attacks until all the German soldiers facing him had been killed. Montgomery's stance shattered the German negotiators' flimsy hopes of securing, at least in this region, a salvation from looming Soviet captivity. Disheartened, they returned to Flensburg to discuss their response with Dönitz and German Armed Forces Commander-in-Chief Field Marshal Wilhelm Keitel.

The Germans arrived back at Montgomery's headquarters on the afternoon of Friday May 4. At 6:30 pm in an inconspicuous canvas tent, on a standard army table covered with a rough blanket for this momentous occasion, Grand Admiral Hans von Friedeberg signed an instrument of surrender. By this instrument he capitulated to the British the 1.7 million German troops who faced Montgomery's forces in northwestern Germany and Denmark, with effect from 8:00 am on May 5. In his moment of triumph, a gloating Montgomery entered the wrong date on the historic surrender document, and had to initial his amendment.

After this surrender, the Western Allies still had to resolve the issue of the capitulation of the remaining German forces deployed along the Western Front. During May 5, and into the next morning, the negotiating German officers dragged their feet to buy time for German units then still fighting the Soviets to retreat west in small groups to enter Western Allied captivity. Meanwhile, on the afternoon of May 5, General von Blaskowitz surrendered the encircled German forces in northwestern Holland to the Canadian army, while on the next day, the German Army Group G deployed in western Austria capitulated to the Americans.

Then, on May 6, Colonel-General Alfred Jodl, Chief of the Armed Forces Operations Staff, flew from Flensburg to Supreme Allied Commander Dwight Eisenhower's headquarters at Rheims, where the latter expected him to sign the immediate unconditional surrender of all remaining German forces to the four Allied powers. Initially, Jodl tried to negotiate only the surrender of those German forces still facing west, excluding those on the Eastern Front. In response, Eisenhower threatened to abandon the negotiations and close the Western Front to all Germans soldiers attempting to surrender, unless Jodl immediately agreed to the unconditional surrender of all Germans forces in all theaters. Jodl radioed Dönitz for instructions, and received his reluctant permission to sign. At 2:41 am on May 7, 1945, Jodl signed the instrument of surrender, which was slated to take effect on May 8 at 11:01 pm British Standard Time. The Germans used the remaining 44 hours before World War II in Europe officially ended to withdraw as many forces as possible from the east and surrender them to the Western Allies.

Finally, in Berlin at 11:30 pm on May 8, after the cessation of hostilities deadline had passed, von Friedeberg and Keitel again signed the instrument of surrender concluded at Rheims the previous morning to confirm the laying down of German arms. Officially, World War II in Europe was over. Dönitz's government continued to function until May 23, when it was dissolved and the second Führer arrested. Subsequently, the Nuremberg War Crimes Tribunal sentenced Dönitz to 10 years' imprisonment. Despite the official German surrender on May 8, though, many German units in the east continued to resist the Soviets during the next few days. Indeed, the very last German forces did not surrender until May 15, 1945, a full week after Germany's official surrender. But by this date, it is fair to say that both the 1944–45 Northwest Europe campaign, and the entire World War II in Europe, had finally ended.

At 11:30 pm on May 8, 1945, in Berlin, once the deadline for the cessation of hostilities agreed the previous day had passed, Field Marshal Keitel signed the confirmatory German instrument of surrender. The supposed Thousand-Year Nazi Reich had, in fact, lasted only a little over a decade. (AKG Berlin)

"The most devastating and costly war"

On May 23, 1945, 15 days after Germany's unconditional surrender, the Allies dissolved Dönitz's residual government. From that point, the German state, in effect, had ceased to exist, and instead the Western Allies and the Soviets established interim military occupation administrations based on the territory they had liberated by the end of the war. This situation lasted until July when, at the Potsdam International Conference, the "Big Four" – America, Britain, France, and the Soviet Union – confirmed earlier agreements to establish

four separate occupation zones within a territorially reduced German state. The conference ceded German territory east of the Oder–Neisse River line, plus southern East Prussia, to the re-established Polish state, and the northern part of East Prussia to the Soviet Union. Elsewhere, Germany returned to its 1936 boundaries, which meant the restoration of an independent Austria and the return of Bohemia-Moravia to a reconstituted Czechoslovakia; in addition, the French temporarily acquired the Saar industrial region.

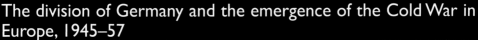

The division of Germany and the emergence of the Cold War in Europe, 1945–57

Berlin: Divided into four national occupation zones 1945–49; West Berlin became part of the German Federal Republic in 1949, despite being entirely within the Soviet-controlled German Democratic Republic.

NORTHERN EAST PRUSSIA

Kaliningrad (Königsberg)

Gdansk (Danzig)

SOUTHERN EAST PRUSSIA

POMERANIA

SOVIET OCCUPATION ZONE 1945–49

SOVIET UNION

THE NETHERLANDS

BRITISH OCCUPATION ZONE

Berlin

Warsaw

GERMAN DEMOCRATIC REPUBLIC (from 1949)

POLAND

BELGIUM

Bonn

Rhine

Elbe

Neisse

Oder

SILESIA

Prague

AMERICAN OCCUPATION ZONE 1945–49

CZECHOSLOVAKIA

0   100 miles

0   200 km

N

Saar

Alsace-Lorraine

FRENCH OCCUPATION ZONE

Vienna

SOVIET ZONE

Danube

FRANCE

AMERICAN ZONE

HUNGARY

ROMANIA

SWITZERLAND   FRENCH ZONE

BRITISH ZONE

1. Eupen-Malmédy: Annexed by Germany from Belgium in 1940; returned to Belgium in 1945.
2. Luxembourg: Annexed by Germany in 1940; restored as an independent state in 1945.
3. Saar region of Germany: To France 1945–57.
4. Alsace-Lorraine: Annexed by Germany from France in 1940; returned to France in 1945.

YUGOSLAVIA

German Federal Republic from 1949; joined NATO 1955
Reconstituted Yugoslav state
Reconstituted Polish state
Parts of pre-1939 Germany ceded to Poland
Parts of pre-1939 Germany ceded to Soviet Union
Warsaw Pact zones

At the Potsdam International Conference in July 1945, the four victorious major Allied powers – "the Big Four" – agreed to the postwar division of Europe. Here Churchill and American President Truman pose for the press. The conference agreed that Germany should return to its pre-1936 boundaries, and be divided temporarily into four national Allied occupation zones. The quadripartite Allied Control Commission in Berlin administered the country. (IWM BN 8944)

Germany. As these cooperative arrangements unfolded, however, the Soviet Union simultaneously began creating Communist satellite regimes in the territories it had liberated, namely Poland, Czechoslovakia, Hungary, Romania, and Bulgaria.

As the four Allied powers began their administration of Germany, they found the country in a ruinous condition. During the last months of the war, seven million Germans had fled from the east to the Reich's western *Länder* to escape the Soviet advance. In the weeks following the German surrender, a further three million either fled or were expelled from Communist-controlled areas into the western occupation zones. These refugees, together with the two million displaced persons already in the three western occupation zones, created a vast administrative burden for the Western Allies. If this was not bad enough, all four Allied powers had also to deal with some nine million former prisoners and slave-laborers then located within the Reich, who required repatriation back to their original countries.

As 50 percent of German housing had been destroyed by May 1945, the Allies had to improvise vast refugee and internment camps to house these displaced persons, plus five million surrendered service personnel. Any German house lucky enough still to possess an intact roof in June 1945, for example, soon came to house several dozen inhabitants in exceedingly cramped conditions, while many families had to live in the cellars of bombed-out dwellings. Not surprisingly, conditions both in these camps and in German towns were often rudimentary, and for most Germans during late 1945 the best they could hope for was to subsist.

To make matters worse, by May 1945 Germany's industrial centers had been so smashed by protracted Allied strategic bombing that production remained at just 15 percent of prewar levels. The combination of this destruction with the devastated German transport system and the masses of displaced persons meant that in late 1945 the production and distribution of food and goods within Germany proved extremely difficult.

This quadripartite Allied administrative division of Germany left the Soviets controlling the country's four eastern provinces (*Länder*), the British administering northern Germany, the French southwestern Germany, and the Americans central and southern Germany. In similar fashion, the four victorious powers also divided the German capital, Berlin – now entirely within Soviet-controlled eastern Germany – into four separate sectors, the Soviet zone being in the east of the city. Berlin housed the Allied Control Commission, the supreme executive power in Germany. The Potsdam Conference also guaranteed access routes from the Western Allied occupation zones into West Berlin by air, road, and rail. Last, the Allies also established four similar occupation zones in a reconstituted Austrian state detached from

The Allies had strictly to ration whatever meager food supplies remained available to prevent major shortages, and so hunger visited many Germans during the second half of 1945. The delivery of food parcels by the International Red Cross saved the lives of many thousands of destitute Germans, yet despite such efforts, the poor living conditions led to the outbreak of several epidemics that cost the lives of several thousand already malnourished individuals.

Not surprisingly, during summer 1945 it was not just the German economy, but that of the whole of Europe, that bore the terrible scars of the previous five years of war. Total industrial production across the continent during 1946, for example, was just one-third of that in 1938, while European food production remained just one half of its prewar levels. The French economy had declined by one half by 1946, compared to 1938, while that of the Soviet Union had slipped by 13 percent. Indeed, it would take much of Europe until the late 1950s to recover from the disruptions caused by the war.

One of the few "winners" of the war, however, was the United States, whose economy proved capable of taking advantage of the disrupted international trade flows, and thus grew by some 50 percent during 1941–45. This boom enabled the Americans, from late 1947, to pump $13 billion of Marshall Aid into Europe to rebuild the shattered continent, as part of the Truman Doctrine that offered support to democratic peoples around the world.

The Marshall Aid scheme epitomized the extent to which the international politico-economic influence of Britain and France had declined through their prosecution of World War II, and how much that of America had grown. Indeed, during the 1950s it was clear that there were now just two superpowers – the Americans and Soviets. Of course, it would take years for the former European colonial powers fully to recognize their own decline – with Britain, for example, only doing so after the humiliation of the abortive 1956 Suez intervention. Undoubtedly, the costs of the war, the contribution made by the colonies,

The vast destruction and dislocation inflicted on the Reich during the last months of the war left the victorious Allies with an immense burden: how to feed the millions of German refugees and displaced persons. Here, British troops supervise the distribution of food to hungry German refugees. (Imperial War Museum BN 2698)

and the puncturing of the myth of the "white man's superiority" all fostered powerful anticolonial insurgencies during 1946–67 that hastened the European powers' "retreat from empire."

Meanwhile, for the German people during 1945–49, their fate lay entirely in the hands of the occupying powers, since their state had effectively ceased to exist. Although at Potsdam the four Allied powers had agreed to execute uniformly the principles that underpinned their occupation – demilitarization, deNazification, deindustrialization, decentralization, and democratization – the implementation of these tenets varied enormously between the zones. These differences increased during 1946–48, as the cooperation evident in late 1945 between East and West degenerated into suspicion.

In the three western-controlled sectors of Germany, the locals generally encountered a severe, but largely reasonable administration. However, some interned German military personnel received fairly harsh treatment, for in the emotive last period of the war not even the Western Allies proved immune from the desire for vengeance on the vanquished Nazi regime. The American Treasury Secretary Hans Morgenthau, for example, suggested deindustrializing Germany completely to prevent it ever again being capable of waging aggressive war, while British Prime Minister Winston Churchill suggested summarily executing 100,000 leading Nazis. In reality, such excesses did not occur in the western occupation zone.

In the Soviet-controlled sector, however, the life of ordinary Germans was extremely harsh. Such severity was not surprising, given the terrible privations that the Soviets had suffered during the war, and the heinous occupation policies that the Germans had implemented within Nazi-occupied Soviet territory. Understandably, the Soviets wished to extract recompense for these losses when they occupied eastern Germany, and so implemented a *de facto* reparations policy by either shipping industrial plants back

east, or else systematically exploiting them *in situ* for the benefit of the Soviet state. This policy, which breached several Allied understandings, was one of the principal reasons for the growing division that emerged between the Western Allies and Soviets during 1947. The ruthlessness with which the Soviets exploited their zone in Germany certainly caused many thousands of Germans to succumb to disease brought about by malnutrition and physical hardship.

Another facet of the Allied administration of Germany was deNazification, the process of both "cleansing" the German people of the "disease" of Nazism and seeking justice for the terrible crimes committed by the Nazis. The most prominent part of this process was the indicting of German war criminals in the Nuremberg International Tribunal. This court prosecuted 22 senior German political and military leaders on the counts of conspiracy to conduct aggressive war, crimes against peace, war crimes, and crimes against humanity. The third count revolved around the barbarous German war-fighting methods seen especially in the east, while count four related mainly to the genocidal policies of the Holocaust that destroyed the majority of Europe's Jewish population, some 5.5 million human beings. After an 11-month trial, the court sentenced 12 of the defendants to death, and three to life imprisonment, while also condemning the Gestapo and SS as criminal organizations.

In addition to the high-profile Nuremberg proceedings, during 1945–47 the Western Allies carried out thousands of de-Nazification hearings against lesser figures, including members of the criminal organizations condemned at Nuremberg. At these hearings, convicted individuals received sentences of one or two years in a deNazification camp. In contrast, Soviet courts in this period sentenced, in rather arbitrary fashion, several million German prisoners of war to the standard Stalinist "tenner" – 10 years' forced labor in the infamous camps of the Gulag Archipelago. Only 60 percent of these German prisoners survived their "tenner" to return to Germany in the mid-1950s.

The Nuremberg process epitomized the desire evident within the "Big Four" during 1945–46 to establish effective Allied cooperation that would help produce a new, more stable, international environment. The Allies' creation of the United Nations (UN) in June 1945, with an initial membership of 50 states, encapsulated this desire. Replacing the defunct League of Nations, this organization sought to help states peacefully resolve their differences, thus saving mankind from the "scourge of war." In addition, the UN would help promote international economic development and the spread of democratization. Such efforts mirrored those undertaken in the wake of the "total wars" of 1792–1815 and 1914–18 to create international institutions that would help promote peace and prosperity. While the UN has had its failures, in the decades since 1945 the organization has clearly contributed to ensuring a more stable and prosperous international system.

During 1946–47, however, the effective cooperation evident in late 1945 between the Western Allies and their Soviet partners over both the founding of the UN and the administration of Germany degenerated into mistrust. This was epitomized by Churchill's

March 1946 warning that an "Iron Curtain" was coming down over Soviet-occupied eastern Europe. As the Soviets tightened their grip on eastern Germany to create a Communist satellite state, the Western Allies increased their cooperation until their three zones coalesced into one entity, termed "Trizonia." To help this entity and the other democratic states of western Europe recover their economic vibrancy so that they could resist the threat of Communism, from late 1947 the Americans began to pump Marshall Aid funds into western Europe.

The 1948 Berlin Blockade, during which the Soviets tried to block access to West Berlin, permanently severed any prospects, however remote, of continuing cooperation over Germany. The blockade now pushed the rapidly emerging division of Germany into western and Soviet-controlled zones into a formalized status. During 1949 these areas became *de facto* independent states – the German Federal and Democratic Republics,

At the Nuremberg International Tribunal, 22 senior German political and military leaders – including Karl Dönitz, Hermann Göring, Alfred Jodl, and Wilhelm Keitel – were tried for the crimes that the Nazi Third Reich had committed over the previous 12 years. Both Jodl and Keitel were subsequently executed for their complicity in the terrible crimes committed by the Nazi regime. (AKG Berlin)

respectively – better known as West and East Germany. Each of these states, however, refused to recognize the existence of the other and both aimed for an eventual reunification of Germany – an ambition not achieved until the end of the Cold War in 1989–90.

Subsequently, during the 1950–53 Korean War, western Europe began to rehabilitate West Germany politically and militarily as a bulwark against the military threat offered by the Communist Warsaw Pact. This process culminated in 1955 with the admission of the German Federal Republic into the North Atlantic Treaty Organization (NATO), the anti-Communist European collective security organization formed in April 1949. The Soviets followed suit by rebuilding East Germany to serve the needs of the Warsaw Pact.

The specter of a Third World War in Europe, therefore, forced both the East and West during 1949–55 to reconstruct their respective parts of the devastated pariah postwar German state. This led directly to the West German "economic miracle" of the 1960s, a process that – after German reunification in 1990 – helped Germany emerge as the dominant economic force within early twenty-first-century Europe. Clearly, the consequences of a "total war" such as that of 1939–45 are both complex and long lasting.

All in all, World War II in Europe was the most devastating and costly war ever fought. Some 55 million human beings perished in a conflagration that sucked in no fewer than 56 states, excluding colonial possessions. During the five-year conflict, Germany incurred 2.8 million military and 2 million civilian deaths, including 550,000 by Western Allied strategic bombing. The Soviets suffered the worst, with 6.3 million military and perhaps 17 million civilian deaths. Europe's other populations suffered a further 1.8 million military and 10.5 million civilian deaths, the latter including 5.5 million Jews. The three Western Allied powers incurred 700,000 military deaths in the European theater. Financially, too, the burden of the war was crippling, with all the belligerents spending some £326 billion ($1.3 trillion) at 1946 prices – equivalent to £2,608 billion ($6.1 trillion) at 1980 prices – in prosecuting the conflict.

Whatever the enormity of the victory achieved in stopping Hitler's heinous Nazi regime, it is clear that the price of this triumph was so that high that it would take many of the alleged "victors" of the war decades to recover from the uniquely appalling experience that was World War II in Europe.

Glossary

AFV Armored Fighting Vehicle.

attenuated Weakened in force or effect.

attritional warfare A military tactic in which to win a war one's enemy must be worn down to the point of collapse through continuous losses in personnel and equipment.

audacity Rude or disrespectful behavior.

becage Terrain that is woodland, pasture, and banks of dense hedgerows interspersed with trees.

bridgehead A strong position secured by an army inside enemy territory from which to advance or attack.

capitulation The act of surrendering.

Commonwealth British Commonwealth (British Empire), also known as the Dominions (Australia, Canada, Newfoundland, New Zealand, South Africa, British Indian Empire, and the Irish Free State).

conscription Required enlistment in the armed forces.

contingents Groups of people united by a common feature, forming part of a larger group (for example, Poles fighting with the British, but at the time that their country was occupied by Germany).

deleterious Causing harm or damage.

deterrent A thing that discourages or is intended to discourage someone from doing something.

disabuse Persuade someone that an idea or belief is mistaken.

ersatz Made or used as a substitute; not real.

flak gun Aircraft defense gun.

Führer German for "leader"; the title assumed by Adolf Hitler in 1934.

husband To conserve or use resources economically.

inculcate To instill or teach an idea by persistent instruction.

interdiction The impeding of an enemy force by aerial bombing of lines of communication or supply.

juggernaut A huge, powerful and overwhelming force.

Kriegsmarine The name of the German navy, 1939–45.

lodgment A temporary defensive work made on a captured part of an enemy's fortification to secure a position and provide protection.

obdurate Stubbornly refusing to change one's opinion or course of action.

ordnance Military weapons and equipment.

parity The state or condition of being equal.

repudiate Deny the truth or validity of.

retrenchment Reduction of costs or spending in response to economic difficulty.

riposte A retaliatory action or maneuver.

rue Bitterly regret something that one has done or allowed to happen.

salient An outward bulge in a line of military attack or defense.

strafe To attack repeatedly with bombs or machine-gun fire from low-flying aircraft.

virulent Bitterly hostile.

V1 rocket A German unmanned, unguided flying bomb, an early version of a cruise missile. The V stands for *Vergeltungswaffe* or "retaliation weapon" (also called Vengeance rocket). The Germans used the V1 in southern England.

Westheer The German army that fought on the Western front.

For More Information

Franklin D. Roosevelt Presidential Library and Museum
4079 Albany Post Road
Hyde Park, NY 12538
(800) FDR-VISIT (800-337-8474)
Web site: http://www.fdrlibrary.marist.edu
The presidential library of Franklin D. Roosevelt houses historical papers, books, and memorabilia collected during FDR's lifetime, including during World War II.

National D-Day Memorial Foundation
P.O. Box 77
Bedford, VA 24523
(800) 351-DDAY
Web site: http://www.dday.org
This organization maintains the National D-Day Memorial in Bedford, Virginia. Tours of the memorial are available, along with educational programs about the lessons and legacy of D-Day; a photo gallery of the monument can be viewed at the Web site.

National World War II Museum
945 Magazine Street
New Orleans, LA 70130
(504) 527-6012
Web site: http://www.nationalww2museum.org
The National World War II Museum opened on June 6, 2000, to honor the Americans who took part in the conflict.

U.S. Army Heritage and Education Center (USAHEC)
950 Soldiers Drive
Carlisle, PA 17013-5021
(717) 245-3419
Web site: http://www.carlisle.army.mil/ahec
The center's mission is to educate the public about the heritage of the army and making records and artifacts available for research. There is an online catalog available for researching topics involving World War II and individual battles.

U.S. National Archives and Records Administration (NARA)
8601 Adelphi Road
College Park, MD 20740-6001
(866) 272-6272
Web site: http://www.archives.gov/research/alic/reference/military/ww2.html
As the country's record keeper, the NARA preserves and makes available valuable records of the U.S. government, including significant electronic documents. Military resources of World War II are provided on the NARA Resources Web page.

World War II Memorial
National Park Service
U.S. Department of the Interior
c/o National Mall and Memorial Parks
900 Ohio Drive SW
Washington, DC 20024
(202) 426-6841
Web site: http://www.nps.gov/nwwm
The World War II Memorial is situated along the central area of the National Mall, between the Washington Monument and the Lincoln Memorial, at the eastern end of the Reflecting Pool along Seventeenth Street.

Web Sites

Due to the changing nature of Internet links, Rosen Publishing has developed an online list of Web sites related to the subject of this book. This site is updated regularly. Please use this link to access this list:

http://www.rosenlinks.com/wweh/nort

For Further Reading

Adams, Simon. *World War II* (DK Eyewitness Books). Revised ed. New York, NY: DK Publishing, 2007.

Altman, Linda Jacobs. *Adolf Hitler: Evil Mastermind of the Holocaust* (Holocaust Heroes and Nazi Criminals). Berkeley Heights, NJ: Enslow Publishers, 2005.

Conway, John Richard. *Primary Source Accounts of World War II* (America's Wars Through Primary Sources). Berkeley Heights, NJ: Enslow Publishers, 2006.

Fenby, Jonathan. *Alliance: The Inside Story of How Roosevelt, Stalin, and Churchill Won One War and Began Another.* New York, NY: Pocket Books, 2006.

Fiscus, James W., ed. *Critical Perspectives on World War II* (Critical Anthologies of Nonfiction Writing). New York, NY: Rosen Publishing, 2005.

Humphrey, Robert E. *Once Upon a Time in War: The 99th Division in World War II* (Campaigns and Commanders). Vol. 18. Norman, OK: University of Oklahoma Press, 2008.

Isserman, Maurice. *World War II* (America at War) 13 Volumes. Updated edition. New York, NY: Chelsea House Publishers, 2003.

Lyons, Michael J. *World War II: A Short History.* 5th ed. Upper Saddle River, NY: Prentice Hall, 2009.

Nardo, Don. *World War II* (Opposing Viewpoints in World History). Farmington Hills, MI: Greenhaven Press, 2004.

Rees, Laurence. *WWII Behind Closed Doors: Stalin, the Nazis, and the West.* New York, NY: Pantheon Books, 2009.

Stein, R. Conrad. *The World War II D-Day Invasion in American History* (In American History). Berkeley Heights, NJ: Enslow Publishers, 2004.

Wagner, Margaret E., Linda Barrett Osborne, Susan Reyburn, and staff of the Library of Congress. *The Library of Congress World War II Companion.* New York, NY: Simon & Schuster, 2007.

World War II: The Definitive Visual History. From Blitzkrieg to Atomic Bomb. New York, NY: DK Publishing, 2009.

Bibliography

Unpublished primary sources

Cabinet Office (CAB) and War Office (WO) Papers, The Public Records Office, Kew.
    Enemy Document Series (EDS) and Field Marshal B. L. Montgomery [BLM] Papers, Department of Documents, Imperial War Museum, London.

Published primary sources

Bradley, O. N., *A Soldier's Story*, New York, 1951.

de Guingand, Maj.-Gen. F., *Operation Victory*, London, 1947.

Eisenhower, D. D., *Crusade in Europe*, New York, 1948.

Montgomery, B. L., *Normandy to the Baltic*, London, 1947.

Patton, G. S., *War as I Knew It*, Boston, 1947.

Speidel, H., *We Defended Normandy*, London, 1951.

Secondary sources

Balkoski, J., *Beyond the Bridgehead*, Harrisburg, PA, 1989.

Blumenson, M., *Breakout and Pursuit*, Washington, DC, 1961.

Blumenson, M., *The Duel for France, 1944*, Boston, 1963.

Carrell, P. (pseud.) [Paul Karl Schmidt], *Invasion They're Coming!*, London, 1962.

D'Este, C., *Decision in Normandy: The Unwritten Story of Montgomery and the Allied Campaign*, London, 1983.

Doubler, M., *Closing with the Enemy: How GIs Fought the War in Europe*, Lawrence, KA, 1994.

Ellis, Maj. L. F., *Victory in the West*, 2 vols, London, 1960, 1968.

English, J. A., *The Canadian Army and the Normandy Campaign: A Study in the Failure of High Command*, London, 1991.

Hamilton, N., *Monty*, 3 vols, London, 1982–86.

Harrison, G., *Cross Channel Attack*, Washington, DC, 1951.

Hart, R. A., *Clash of Arms: How the Allies Won in Normandy*, Boulder, CO, 2001.

Hart, R. A., "Feeding Mars: the role of logistics in the German defeat in Normandy, 1944," *War in History*, vol. 3, no. 4 (Fall 1996), pp. 418–35.

Hart, S. A., *Montgomery and "Colossal Cracks": The 21st Army Group in Northwest Europe, 1944–45*, Westport, CT, 2000.

Hart, S. A., "Montgomery, morale, casualty conservation and 'colossal cracks': 21st Army Group operational technique in north-west Europe 1944–45," in B. H. Reid (ed.), *Fighting Power*, London, 1995.

Hastings, M., *Overlord: D-Day and the Battle of Normandy*, London, 1984.

Horne, A. and Montgomery, B., *The Lonely Leader: Monty 1944–1945*, London, 1994.

Keegan, J., *Six Armies in Normandy*, New York, 1982.

Kershaw, R. J., *It Never Snows in September: The German View of Market Garden and the Battle of Arnhem, September 1944*, Ramsbury, England, 1990.

Lamb, R., *Montgomery in Europe 1943–45: Success or Failure?*, London, 1983.

Ryan, C., *The Longest Day*, London, 1960.

Schulman, M., *Defeat in the West*, London, 1968.

Stacey, Col. C. P., *The Victory Campaign*, Ottawa, 1960.

Thompson, R. W., *Montgomery the Field Marshal: A Critical Study*, London, 1969.

Weigley, R. F., *Eisenhower's Lieutenants: The Campaigns of France and Germany 1944–5*, 2 vols, London, 1981.

Whitaker, W. D. and Whitaker, S., *The Battle of the River Scheldt*, London, 1985.

Index

3 2186 00184 3274

About the Authors

Professor Robert O'Neill is the series editor of the Essential Histories. His wealth of knowledge and expertise shapes the series content and provides up-to-the-minute research and theory. Born in 1936 an Australian citizen, he served in the Australian army (1955–68) and has held a number of eminent positions in history circles, including the Chichele Professorship of the History of War at All Souls College, University of Oxford, 1987–2001, and the Chairmanship of the Board of the Imperial War Museum and the Council of the International Institute for Strategic Studies, London, England. He is the author of many books, including works on the German army and the Nazi party, and the Korean and Vietnam wars. Now based in Australia on his retirement from Oxford, he is the Chairman of the Council of the Australian Strategic Policy Institute.

Dr. Russell Hart earned his Ph.D. in 1997 from Ohio State University. He is Associate Professor of History and Program Chair, Diplomacy and Military Studies, at Hawaii Pacific University, Honolulu. He is the co-author of *German Tanks of WWII*; *Weapons and Tactics of the Waffen-SS*; *Panzer: The Illustrated History of Germany's Armored Forces in WWII*, and *The German Solder in WWII*. He is the author of *Clash of Arms: How the Allies Won in Normandy* and *Guderian: Panzer Pioneer or Myth Maker*. He lives in Honolulu, Hawaii.

Dr. Stephen Hart is senior lecturer in the War Studies department, the Royal Military Academy Sandhurst. He is the author of *Montgomery and the "Colossal Cracks": The 21st Army Group in Northwest Europe 1944* and *Sherman Firefly vs. Tiger: Normandy 1944*. He has also co-authored several popular histories of aspects of the German Army in World War II.

Fossil Ridge Public Library District
Braidwood, IL 60408

Who on Earth is Rachel Carson?
Mother of the Environmental Movement

Read about other Scientists Saving the Earth

Who on Earth is Aldo Leopold?
Father of Wildlife Ecology
ISBN: 978-1-59845-115-3
ISBN: 1-59845-115-4

Who on Earth is Archie Carr?
Protector of Sea Turtles
ISBN: 978-1-59845-120-7
ISBN: 1-59845-120-0

Who on Earth is Rachel Carson?
Mother of the Environmental Movement
ISBN: 978-1-59845-116-0
ISBN: 1-59845-116-2

Who on Earth is Sylvia Earle?
Undersea Explorer of the Ocean
ISBN: 978-1-59845-118-4
ISBN: 1-59845-118-9

Who on Earth is Dian Fossey?
Defender of the Mountain Gorillas
ISBN: 978-1-59845-117-7
ISBN: 1-59845-117-0

Who on Earth is Jane Goodall?
Champion for the Chimpanzees
ISBN: 978-1-59845-119-1
ISBN: 1-59845-119-7

Scientists Saving the Earth

Who on Earth is
Rachel Carson?
Mother of the Environmental Movement

Marty Fletcher and Glenn Scherer

Enslow Publishers, Inc.
40 Industrial Road
Box 398
Berkeley Heights, NJ 07922
USA

http://www.enslow.com

Copyright © 2009 by Enslow Publishers, Inc.

All rights reserved.

No part of this book may be reproduced by any means
without the written permission of the publisher.

Library of Congress Cataloging-in-Publication Data

Scherer, Glenn.
  Who on Earth is Rachel Carson? : mother of the environmental movement / Glenn Scherer and
Marty Fletcher.
      p. cm. — (Scientists saving the Earth)
  Includes bibliographical references and index.
  Summary: "Details the life of Rachel Carson, with chapters devoted to her early years, life, work,
ecological writings, and legacy, as well as how children can follow in her footsteps"—Provided by
publisher.
  ISBN-13: 978-1-59845-116-0
  ISBN-10: 1-59845-116-2
  1. Carson, Rachel, 1907–1964—Juvenile literature. 2. Biologists—United States—Biography—
Juvenile literature. 3. Environmentalists—United States—Biography—Juvenile literature. I. Fletcher,
Marty. II. Title.
  QH31.C33S32 2009
  333.95'16092—dc22
  [B]
                                  2008028498
Printed in the United States of America

10 9 8 7 6 5 4 3 2 1

To Our Readers:
We have done our best to make sure all Internet Addresses in this book were active and appropriate
when we went to press. However, the author and the publisher have no control over and assume no
liability for the material available on those Internet sites or on other Web sites they may link to. Any
comments or suggestions can be sent by e-mail to comments@enslow.com or to the address on the
back cover.

♻ Enslow Publishers, Inc., is committed to printing our books on recycled paper. The paper in every
book contains 10% to 30% post-consumer waste (PCW). The cover board on the outside of each book
contains 100% PCW. Our goal is to do our part to help young people and the environment too!

Photo Credits: Associated Press, p. 10; Clipart®, p.19; Enslow Publishers, Inc., p. 65, 73; National
Archives and Records Administration(NARA), pp. 66–67; Photo courtesy ccbarr, p. 16; Photograph by
Mary Frye, used by permission of the Rachel Carson Council, Inc., p. 37; Photographer John Bortniak,
courtesy of the National Oceanic and Atmospheric Administration (NOAA), p. 38; Rachel Carson
Collection, College Archives, Chatham University, p. 30; Regina Greenwood, p. 79; Sarah K. Vogel,
pp. 6–7; ShutterStock®, pp. 40, 48–49, 68; State Archives of Florida, p. 82; U.S. Army Signal Corps,
p. 77; U.S. Fish and Wildlife Service, pp. 53, 61, 63, 84, 89, 94–95; Used by permission of the Rachel
Carson Council, Inc., pp. 14, 16, 25, 27.

Cover Photo: Foreground: Rachel Carson Portrait (U.S. Fish and Wildlife Service);Background:
Landscape (ShutterStock®)

Contents

1

View of Rachel Carson's backyard where she wrote *Silent Spring.*

The Environmental Movement Is Born

> *It is a wholesome and necessary thing for us to turn again to the earth and in the contemplation of her beauties to know of wonder and humility.*
>
> *—Rachel Carson*

—Rachel Carson: A Conservation Legacy

In 1962, Rachel Carson, a scientist and author, published a new book. Known for her books about the sea, this book was different. It was about a war—humanity's war on nature. Specifically, it was about pesticides

and the great harm they were doing to plants, animals, and people.

The book, *Silent Spring*, began with what is probably Rachel Carson's most famous short piece of writing, the "Fable for Tomorrow." In just three pages, Carson laid out an environmental parable for our time. Like other parables, this story was meant to teach a lesson.

The "Fable for Tomorrow" drew a vivid picture of an imaginary town in the heart of America known for its natural bounty. The little town was like many towns across the United States. Neighboring hillsides decked in lush forests of oak, maple, and birch surrounded prosperous farms and orchards. Alder, laurel, and wildflowers lined roads to the delight of travelers who happened upon them.

Wildlife abounded. Fox and deer moved from field to woods foraging for food. Even in winter the town was a place of beauty "where countless birds came to feed on the berries and on the seed heads of the dried weeds rising above the snow," Rachel Carson wrote. "The countryside was, in fact, famous for the abundance and variety of its bird life."[1] She went on to tell how people came long distances just to observe the vast flocks of migrating birds. Other tourists came to fish the clear, cool streams of the town.

"Then a strange blight crept over the area and everything began to change. Some evil spell had settled on the community."[2] Mysterious diseases began to infect the town's farms, sickening and killing chickens, sheep, and cows. New, mysterious, and frightening diseases also appeared among the town's residents. Farmers and their families became sick, and so did the other adults and children who lived in the town.

Most disturbing of all was the deadly silence that fell upon the landscape.

"There was a strange stillness. . . . It was a spring without voices. On the mornings that had once throbbed with the dawn chorus of robins, catbirds, doves, jays, wrens, and scores of other bird voices there was now no sound; only silence lay over the fields and woods and marsh."[3]

The town continued to sicken. No chicks hatched. Pigs bore young, which quickly grew sick and died. Apple trees bloomed, but no bees came to pollinate them, so no fruit grew in the orchards. Withered brown vegetation replaced the roadside wildflowers. The brooks that had attracted fishermen now supported no aquatic life at all. The countryside was lifeless.

The only clue to the strange plague that had befallen the town, its people, its plants, and its animals was a white powder that fell on rooftops, lawns, streams, fields, and woods. "No witchcraft, no enemy

◯ Activist and author Rachel Carson, whose book *Silent Spring* led to the study of pesticides, testified before a Senate Government Operation Subcommittee in Washington, D.C. on June 4, 1963. Carson urged Congress to curb the sale of chemical pesticides and aerial spraying.

action had silenced the rebirth of new life in this stricken world," Carson wrote. "The people had done it themselves."[4]

Then, startlingly, Carson revealed that this was no fable. The disasters that she described have befallen many towns, farms, forests, and streams all across the United States and around the world. "A grim specter has crept upon us almost unnoticed, and this imagined tragedy may easily become a stark reality we all shall know," she concluded.[5]

Carson revealed in *Silent Spring* that the deadly pestilence that had silenced the birds and come quietly into our midst was the indiscriminate spraying of synthetic chemical pesticides.

With *Silent Spring's* appearance in 1962, Rachel Carson, the quiet and unassuming writer and marine biologist, made Americans think about their dependence on nature. Pesticide manufacturers, long seen as helping to control nature, raged at her attack. They assaulted Carson's book and also criticized her scientific facts and her character, calling her a "hysterical woman."[6]

Meanwhile, the millions of people who read *Silent Spring* awoke to discover that the natural world was under assault by DDT and other chemical pesticides. Within a year, public outcry forced many states to begin regulating pesticides, with the federal government following suit shortly.

The pesticide makers continued in their fight against those who now called themselves environmentalists. And remarkably, almost fifty years later, environmentalists are still struggling to protect the natural world from those who seek to control it.

Silent Spring helped mark the birth of the modern environmental movement. Other writers and scientists alerted the public to the dangers of problems such as water pollution, air pollution, urban sprawl and habitat loss, the destruction of the ozone layer, and global warming. "Without this book," former Vice President Al Gore wrote, "the environmental movement might have been delayed or never have developed at all."[7]

Rachel Carson is a hero for our time, a scientist who examined the facts and saw that the natural and human world was in danger. Despite the criticism of those who opposed her, she bravely sounded an alarm. This is her story.

2

The Birth of an Environmentalist

Rachel Carson was born on May 27, 1907, the youngest of three children. She grew up in the tiny town of Springdale, Pennsylvania, about eighteen miles from Pittsburgh near the Allegheny River. When Rachel was born, Springdale was still very much like the little town described at the beginning of *Silent Spring*. It had a population of just 1,199 people, and though a few factories were built there, it was still surrounded by woods, orchards, fields, and meadows. It was the perfect place for a child to fall in love with nature.

Rachel's parents, Robert and Maria Carson, met in the winter of 1893 at a choral music social

Maria Carson and her children Marian, Rachel, and Robert. Rachel was the youngest of the three Carson children.

where they both sang. They courted and were married in 1894. They had their first child in 1897, a daughter named Marian Frazier. A son, Robert, followed in 1899. Marian was ten years old and Robert was eight when Rachel was born. In 1900, the family had moved to the west edge of Springdale.

A Farm at the Edge of Town

The home in which Rachel was born and raised had been built as a log cabin sometime after 1867. By the time Rachel was born, the home had grown from a log cabin to be a two-story clapboard house with four rooms, no central heating, and no indoor plumbing—a tight, cluttered space in which to raise three children. The Carsons did not have much money. Rachel's father moved from job to job. He worked as a clerk, as a traveling salesman, and eventually at a local electric power plant.

From the very beginning, Rachel escaped from the crowded house into her parents' sixty-four-acre farm that she loved to explore. A barn and stable, springhouse, chicken coop, and two out-buildings that the family used as their bathroom stood behind the house. The peacefulness of the farm with its large kitchen garden, lilac bushes, maple trees, and apple and peach orchards contrasted sharply with the bustling household and the growing businesses of Springdale.

⟐The Rachel Carson Homestead in Springdale, Pennsylvania, as it appeared at the time of Rachel Carson's 100th Birthday Celebration.

As a child, Rachel helped take care of the family's farm animals. Though the automobile had been invented and cars were already on the streets of Springdale, the Carson family was too poor to own one. They had a horse and buggy instead. The family also raised chickens, pigs, and kept many dogs, which were Rachel's constant companions on her nature walks.

Rachel's First Mentor

Rachel Carson benefited from some wonderful teachers throughout her life. Her first great teacher was her mother, Maria. While the older Carson children went off to grammar school and high school in Springdale, Rachel spent her first five years alone all day with her mother. Even after Rachel started school, her mother would often keep her at home for long periods of time whenever the flu or other illnesses broke out in the community. But that didn't mean that Rachel wasn't learning.

Rachel's mother loved music and books, and she introduced her daughter to the world of literature. Rachel's mother also introduced her to nature, leading many short jaunts over the countryside.

Mother and daughter especially loved birding. They used the *Handbook of Nature Study,* published in 1911, to identify birds, other animals, plants, and even insects on their farm. Author Anna Comstock wrote: "Nature-study is an effort to make the individual use his senses instead of losing them; to train him to keep his eyes open to all things so that his powers of discrimination shall be based on wisdom."[1] Rachel Carson took this instruction to heart, becoming a keen observer of wild things.

🔵 Rachel Carson as a child, reading to her dog, Candy.

Note that the passage from Anna Comstock's book, even though written by a woman, refers only to "him" in regard to nature study. There is no mention of girls taking part in the activity. At that time, and throughout Rachel Carson's life, she would have to battle this "gender bias," where only boys and men were expected to become naturalists and biologists. Women were expected to take care of the home and children.

Still, Comstock's book proved invaluable. It featured dozens of lessons, such as how to identify cardinals and grosbeaks, the life habits of snapping turtles and skunks, and the techniques for observing butterflies and other insects.

A Love for Reading and Writing

Rachel also loved reading. She liked stories that featured animals. Rachel was fond of the author Beatrix Potter, who wrote *Peter Rabbit,* and Kenneth Grahame, who wrote the *Wind in the Willows.* These stories treated

🔵 Peter Rabbit Illustration

the animals in them as if they were people. The animals often wore clothes, drove cars, and thought and talked like people did.

Rachel learned from what she read, and soon she began to write too. "I read a great deal almost from infancy," she remembered later in life, "and I suppose I must have realized someone wrote the books, and thought it would be fun to make up stories too."[2]

Around age eight, Rachel wrote her first story called "The Little Brown House." In that story two wrens, named Mr. Wren and Jenny Wren, fly across the countryside seeking a home. They at last find a pretty brown birdhouse with a green roof in which to live. In a later version of this story, Rachel began to move away from treating animals like people, and instead she described how the wrens really behaved in nature.

As she grew older, Rachel wandered alone through the family orchards and over the family's acreage and became a keen observer of wildlife, especially becoming expert in the identification of birds.

Writing for St. Nicholas Magazine

In 1873, *St. Nicholas Magazine,* was first published. Even today it is considered to be one of the finest magazines ever created for children. The magazine's

editor, Mary Mapes Dodge, set out her editorial policy: ". . . To foster a love of country, home, nature, truth, beauty, and sincerity. . . . To give reading matter which every parent may pass to his children unhesitatingly."[3]

St. Nicholas Magazine featured many articles, stories, and poems written by adults for children. But the magazine also included a section called the *St. Nicholas League,* works written by children themselves. *St. Nicholas Magazine* helped launched the careers of many famous authors, including William Faulkner, F. Scott Fitzgerald, e.e. cummings, Edna St. Vincent Millay, and E. B. White. It also helped launch Rachel Carson's career as a published writer.

In 1918, eleven-year-old Rachel Carson entered the pages of *St. Nicholas Magazine* with her first story, "A Battle in the Clouds." This World War I story told of a Canadian aviator killed while flying over the battlefield of France. The story was a retelling of one her brother, Robert, had written home to the Carson family during his days in the Army Air Service.

Rachel became a regular contributor to *St. Nicholas Magazine,* offering two more World War I stories to the magazine in 1918 and 1919. Her fourth story, "A Famous Sea-Fight," was a tale from the Spanish-American War, and told about the victory of Admiral Dewey over the Spanish in Manila Bay.

Her last published story in *St. Nicholas Magazine* was her first nature piece for the magazine. In it, fourteen-year-old Rachel used her own personal experiences rather than secondhand historical events. "My Favorite Recreation" told the story of a day out rambling over the Carson's farm:

> The call of the trail on that dewy May morning was too strong to resist. The sun was barely an hour high when Pal [my dog] and I set off for a day of our favorite sport with a lunch box, a canteen, a note-book and a camera. Your experienced woods-man will say that we are going birds'-nesting—in the most approved fashion.
>
> Soon our trail turned aside into deeper woodland. It wound up a gently sloping hill, carpeted with fragrant pine needles. It was our own discovery, Pal's and mine, and the fact gave us a thrill of exul-tation. It was the sort of place that awes you by its majestic silence, interrupted only by the rustling breeze and the distant tinkle of water. . . .
>
> Countless discoveries made the day memorable: the bob-white's nest, tightly packed with eggs, the oriole's cradle, the framework of sticks the cuckoo calls a nest, and the lichen-covered home of the humming-bird.
>
> Late in the afternoon a penetrating "Teacher! teacher! TEACHER!" reached our ears. An oven-bird! A careful search revealed his nest, a little round ball of grass, securely hidden on the ground.

The cool of approaching night settled. The wood-thrushes trilled their golden melody. The setting sun transformed the sky into a sea of blue and gold.

A vesper-sparrow sang his evening lullaby. We turned slowly homeward, gloriously tired, gloriously happy![4]

In this piece, we see qualities in Carson's writing that would appear again and again in later years. She possessed an eye for elegant detail—"the bob-white's nest, tightly packed eggs"—and a reverence and love for nature. There is a playfulness in the writing as well, but the anthropomorphizing that was found in her earliest attempts at writing has disappeared—the birds talk with their own natural voices, not with the voices of people. We see the first glimmers of the expert naturalist and scientist in her writing.

Learning by Example and From Her Surroundings

Rachel didn't just learn from reading and writing. Her parents taught her strong environmental values. For example, when a mining company tried to buy the mineral rights for the farm in order to dig a coal mine underneath it, Rachel's father refused to sell. The family could have used the money but he feared that the coal company's tunneling might damage the natural beauty of the land.

Rachel's mother showed similar concerns. When she found an insect inside the family home she didn't kill it. Instead she gently captured it and released it outdoors. Whenever her small children came home carrying natural treasures, she would encourage them to take the bird nests, acorns, and other artifacts back into the woods and place them where they had found them.

Rachel also saw what happens to nature when the human population increases rapidly and development takes place with little or no control. Between 1910 and 1920, the population of Springdale more than doubled. As Rachel grew older, the town grew more industrial, dirtier, and more polluted. New homes and factories replaced woods, fields, and orchards. Iron furnaces polluted the air, and boats plied the Allegheny River hauling iron ore, oil, logs, and coal. The people who came to Springdale were forced to endure the stench of the glue factory, and in later years, the soot from two coal-fired power plants at either end of the village.

Rachel never forgot the sad transformation of her rural hometown into an industrial working-class community, nor did she forget the damage such uncontrolled changes did to the animals, birds, and plants she loved.

⬆ Rachel, Robert (in Army/Air Service uniform), and Marion about 1919.

High School

Rachel graduated from Springdale Elementary School, but her parents could not afford the regular train fare needed to send her to nearby Allegheny High School. So Rachel stayed at her grammar school for her freshman and sophomore years, being tutored in high-school-level classes. Things continued to go poorly for the Carsons financially, and they were sometimes unable to pay their mounting bills. Marian and Robert both dropped out of high school, and both struggled to make a living.

Rachel was able to attend her junior and senior years of high school in the town of Parnassus, two miles from Springdale, and commuted there by trolley. Her mother helped pay her way by offering piano lessons to Springdale children. In high school, Rachel became very involved in sports, playing basketball and field hockey, and cheering at pep rallies for the Parnassus football team. She graduated in 1925 at the age of eighteen.

Next to her photo in her high-school yearbook the following lines appeared describing Rachel:

Rachel's like the mid-day sun
Always very bright
Never stops her studying
'Til she gets it right.[5]

Rachel at the time of her graduation from Parnassus High School in 1925.

Setting Course for the Future

Rachel Carson's childhood gave her a firm foundation for her later life. From her mother, her first great teacher and constant companion, she learned a reverence for nature, skill in nature observation, a love of reading and studying, and the joy of writing.

Later in life Rachel Carson would say, "I can remember no time, even in earliest childhood, when I didn't assume I was going to be a writer. Also, I can remember no time when I wasn't interested in the out-of-doors and the whole world of nature. Those interests, I know, I inherited from my mother and have always shared with her."[6]

3

The Path to Science

Considering the poor economic circumstances in which Rachel Carson was raised, it seemed unlikely that she could afford to go college. But her studious nature and excellent grades made the possibility of college scholarships a reality.

In 1925, Rachel earned admission to the Pennsylvania College for Women in Pittsburgh [now Chatham College] and won an annual tuition state scholarship of one hundred dollars based on her achievements in high school. The Carsons planned to sell off some of their land in order to afford the eight hundred dollars needed for room and board. Rachel's mother increased the number of piano

Rachel Carson's yearbook photo from the Pennsylvania College for Women, taken in 1928.

students, sold apples, chickens, and the family china in order to help her daughter to attend college. To keep costs down, Rachel and her mother made all of the clothes Rachel wore to school. Still there wasn't enough money to pay all the college bills, but the Carsons were surprised to learn that secret benefactors at the Pennsylvania College for Women had contributed money to help pay the way for their daughter.

Rachel had few friends in college. The confident, quiet, independent young woman often kept to herself, studying constantly. She seldom attended the dances and parties that were often held for the young women students. When she did have free time, her mother often came to visit, and the two solitary figures would walk the campus together or talk in Rachel's room. On the weekends that her mother didn't come to visit, Rachel often took the eighteen-mile train ride home to Springdale. Some of the other students teasingly suggested that because her mother was at the school so often that she too should have to pay tuition.

Choosing a Career

Most young girls attending the Pennsylvania College for Women in the 1920s had little hope of establishing independent careers. They expected to become well-educated wives and mothers. Rachel had little interest in a domestic lifestyle.

She majored in English at first, in hopes of beginning to fulfill her literary goals. Rachel had seen how her own mother—a very well-educated woman—had been saddled by a husband who couldn't make adequate money or provide for his family. So Rachel's sole goal in her first two years of college was to become an independent writer.

Rachel Carson took courses in history, art, sociology, French, physical education, and English composition in hopes of making herself a better, more well-rounded student. But it was the love of nature that triggered her passions. In her first college papers she wrote: "I love all the beautiful things of nature, and the wild creatures are my friends."[1]

English Professor Grace Croff became Rachel's second great teacher and also a close friend. She encouraged Rachel to write short stories and essays using all of her imagination, eye for detail, lyric writing skills, and knowledge of natural history. Rachel wrote term papers and themes, such as "Morning in the Woods," that evoked nature and broadened her understanding of birds and birding.

Rachel practiced her literary skills by writing for *The Arrow*, the student newspaper, and for *The Englicode,* the college literary magazine.

A Fateful Meeting

In 1926, during Rachel's sophomore year of college, she took a course in biology with Professor

Mary Scott Skinker. Though Rachel took this course to fulfill her science requirements for an English degree, it changed her life.

Mary Scott Skinker became Rachel's third mentor, and certainly the most important since her mother had taught her as a child. Skinker expected her students to meet the highest standards, and her biology course was one that many students avoided because it was so difficult. But Rachel loved the challenges. She found that biology and the language of science were the key to natural history she had unknowingly been searching for. Rachel thrived in the classroom, lab work, and later, field studies. She discovered that science added a discipline to her lyrical and poetic literary writings that had been missing in the past. She saw that it provided her with a deeper understanding of the natural world around her.

Skinker found Rachel to be curious, hard working, intelligent, and quick to learn. The two developed a close teacher-student relationship, and within a very short time became close friends. They would stay lifelong friends until Skinker's death in 1948.

Two years into college, Rachel made a fateful decision. She changed her major from English to biology. Such a decision was bold, since at that time the scientific field was dominated by men. Though Rachel realized that it might be difficult

to find a job in science, especially in scientific research, she didn't care. She had discovered that science was her true vocation, and she moved boldly into the science curriculum at the college. Rachel felt sure that if her mentor, Mary Scott Skinker, could get a job teaching science, then she could too.

Falling in Love With the Sea

As a child growing up in landlocked Springdale, Pennsylvania, Rachel Carson never had an opportunity to see the ocean. But when she was still a child, the sea stirred her imagination. Springdale residents tell a story that when Rachel was still a girl, she found the fossil of a sea creature embedded in a rocky outcrop on her family's farm. The discovery electrified her. She wanted to know how the fossil came to be there, what animal made it, and what had happened to turn the farm from seabed into dry land so long ago.

While attending college, Rachel wrote a short story set on the New England coast—a place she had never been. In "The Master of the Ship's Light," she did an unbelievable job of evoking the wonders of the sea, especially considering the fact that she had never seen it. Instead, she relied on her reading of great sea stories like Herman Melville's *Moby Dick* and other books by author Joseph Conrad. Grace Croff told Rachel that her

story was "so good because you have made what might be a relatively technical subject very intelligible to the reader. The use of incident and narrative is particularly good."[2] Here Croff points out a writer's skills that would mark Rachel's later literary work.

Rachel Carson's decision to make the sea her life came while still studying English with Croff. On a stormy night, while rain lashed outside her dorm hall window, Rachel read poet Alfred Lord Tennyson's poem "Locksley Hall." When she read the following lines she knew what she had to do. Tennyson concluded his poem:

> Cramming all the blast before it, in its breast a
>   thunderbolt.
> Let it fall on Locksley Hall, with rain or hail,
>   or fire or snow;
> For the mighty wind arises, roaring seaward,
>   and I go.[3]

In that moment, Rachel Carson sensed that her destiny would be intertwined with the world's wild oceans and their creatures.

Woods Hole

In December 1928, while still an undergraduate at the Pennsylvania College for Women, Rachel Carson applied to the master's science program at Johns Hopkins University in Maryland. Her fine grades in high school and as a college undergraduate helped her to be speedily admitted to the major university's

zoology program. In fact, Rachel Carson was one of only seven applicants whose high scholastic standing earned them a scholarship. Such an honor had rarely been awarded to a woman at that time. She was to report to the university in 1930.

Before going off to Johns Hopkins, however, during the summer of 1929, Rachel Carson was awarded a fellowship at the Woods Hole Marine Biological Laboratory on the Atlantic coast of Massachusetts. For more than a century, Woods Hole has been considered America's premier oceanographic institute. There one would find "[t]he best students from the best universities, the brightest young faculty, the most successful scientists working at the pinnacle of the [marine biology] profession—an unmatched collection of researchers and educators congregates every year in the seaside village whose name has become synonymous with science."[4] It was here at Woods Hole that Rachel Carson first experienced the sea.

For eight glorious weeks in the summer of 1929, Rachel Carson was completely captivated by the sea and by her fellow oceanographic researchers at Woods Hole. As a beginning investigator, she was welcomed into the ranks of her fellow scientists. She was also happy to find that there was no prejudice against women researchers there. Since its founding in 1871, Woods Hole has been famous for treating scientific researchers of

◐ Rachel Carson during her first summer at Woods Hole Biological Laboratory, 1929.

both sexes with full equality. Carson was one of seventy-one beginning investigators that summer, thirty-one of whom were women.

At the laboratory, Carson worked side by side with some of the nation's top scientists. She was able to examine sea creatures, such as living sea urchins and horseshoe crabs, firsthand. She sailed on the Woods Hole research vessel and worked in its labs. Every evening, she ate dinner with all of the other scientists, participating in lively discussions of their research efforts. She joined in parties, picnics, and marine animal and plant specimen collecting trips. Carson also discovered the facility's exceptional library, which featured

scientific journals from around the world. Here she would gather her notes for what would later become her first book, *Under the Sea-Wind.* Here the woman who had grown up in a landlocked Pennsylvania town began to explore the sea that was to be the topic of three of her books.

Rachel Carson was as moved by the poetry of the ocean as she was by the science. When she was

⬆ Rachel Carson first studied at the Marine Biological Laboratory in Woods Hole, Massachusetts, in 1929. She returned there many times as she wrote her eloquent books about the sea. This picturesque seaside town is still a vibrant center for marine research.

at Woods Hole, she would find a large boulder by the sea and watch for hours the play of sun and clouds, waves and tides. She loved the scent of the ocean spray and the sound of the crashing gray waves on the North Atlantic shore. She would spend hours exploring the tidal pools, looking for new organisms among the seaweed, flotsam, and jetsam. One eventful night, during the full moon, she watched the mating ritual of thousands of polychete worms, bristly marine creatures, writhing beneath the murky depths of the waves.

At Woods Hole, Rachel Carson experienced the soft mysticism and beauty of the sea along with hard-edged science. Her brief stay there in 1929 would be the first of many more summers exploring this coast.

On to Johns Hopkins University

Rachel Carson finished her undergraduate studies at the Pennsylvania College for Women in spring 1929. She graduated with honors, and her entire family attended the graduation ceremony.

In the fall, she headed for Johns Hopkins University in Baltimore, to begin work on a master's degree in zoology. When Johns Hopkins University first opened its doors in 1876, its president, Daniel Coit Gilman, set the agenda for the prestigious school. "What are we aiming at?" Gilman asked in his first college speech. "The encouragement of

A sea urchin.

research...and the advancement of individual scholars, who by their excellence will advance the sciences they pursue, and the society where they dwell."[5] By the time Rachel Carson attended the school, it was considered one of the leading scientific research universities in the country.

As Rachel Carson began her studies, the U.S. economy fell into a deep decline, and the nation entered the Great Depression. Tens of millions of Americans were out of work. Still, a big city like Baltimore offered more job opportunities than a little town like Springdale, Pennsylvania, so Rachel Carson moved her family to Maryland to live with her. She found a small house near Johns Hopkins University. The house was crowded, but the family lived in better circumstances than it had in Pennsylvania.

Rachel Carson was especially happy to have her mother again living close by, after nine months of separation—the longest time the two had ever been apart. Maria Carson would play an important role when her daughter began writing articles and books. She would become an important sounding board for her daughter's writing, and would also assist in the day-to-day publishing activities, such as typing up manuscripts.

Carson worked hard at Johns Hopkins, taking on teaching duties to help support her family. In 1930, she became a biology teaching assistant at

the Johns Hopkins summer school, a job she held through 1936. In 1931, she also began teaching at the University of Maryland in College Park. With both of these jobs the Carson family was helped to make ends meet financially.

In 1932, Rachel Carson received her master's degree in marine zoology from Johns Hopkins. She planned to go right on to earn her doctoral degree, but the financial hardships of the Great Depression made this a difficult goal. Family hardships also put pressure on Carson to earn more money. Her sister, Marian, suffered from diabetes and was often too ill to work at her part-time clerical position. Her brother, Robert, was unable to keep a regular job, and her father developed a heart condition that kept him from working.

Finally, early in 1934, Carson gave up her dream of getting a doctoral degree in zoology. She dropped out of Johns Hopkins and began looking for steady work in order to support her family. She continued teaching part-time at the University of Maryland, while searching for a full-time academic teaching position in biology. Unfortunately, at that time most of those positions were given to men and not women.

Science Versus Literature

Throughout Carson's undergraduate studies at the Pennsylvania College for Women and her graduate

studies at Johns Hopkins University, she had struggled to decide between her love of science and her love of writing. A twist of fate at the height of the Great Depression would help Carson realize that she didn't need to make a choice. She could become an eloquent spokesperson for science, a writer of radio programs, reports, brochures, magazine articles, and eventually, books about the sea and the environment.

Eloquent Advocate for the Sea

The lack of scientific positions open to women made it difficult for Rachel Carson to find a position as a biological researcher or a full-time academic. Desperate for a livelihood with which to support her family, she began writing again. She revised some of the poems and short stories she had written in college and began submitting them to magazines. Unfortunately, the *Saturday Evening Post, Collier's, Reader's Digest,* and other popular magazines did not accept her work. All that she was left with for her hard work were rejection slips.

Things became more worrisome when her seventy-one-year-old father died. Robert Carson had been suffering from a heart condition and had been unable to work for a number of years. Then one sunny July morning in 1935, he complained to his wife of not feeling well. She suggested a walk and some fresh air. But Robert Carson had just stepped out the back door of the house when he fell facedown on the lawn. He died moments later of a fatal heart attack.

Promising Employment

Although Carson saw herself as the principal breadwinner for her family, she was unable to get a good research job or teaching position. Her old mentor Mary Scott Skinker urged her to take the civil-service examination, a requirement for getting work with the federal government.

Rachel Carson took three exams, one for junior parasitologist, one for junior wildlife biologist, and one for junior aquatic biologist. She scored well in all three tests, though she still didn't immediately land a full-time job.

Mary Scott Skinker urged Rachel Carson to call on Elmer Higgins, a good friend of hers, who was the head of the U.S. Bureau of Fisheries (later reorganized as the U.S. Fish and Wildlife Service). Carson's character, her academic record, and her civil-service scores impressed Higgins, but he didn't

have any job immediately available for Carson. Instead, he hired her as a writing-consultant on fifty-two seven-minute-long weekly radio shows about marine life entitled *Romance Under the Waters*. Other scientists working for Higgins had tried to do the job but had been unable to make the jump from scientific jargon to language everyone could understand.

This writing-consulting job offer was a turning point in Rachel Carson's career. Suddenly, she was able to bring together her two best skills: her scientific knowledge and her writing ability.

Higgins was thrilled with the first radio script Carson worked on, and he invited her back to write the entire series of radio programs.

Carson realized almost immediately that she had found her niche. She began turning the research from the radio scripts into magazine articles about the marine life of Chesapeake Bay. She sent off one of these essays to the *Baltimore Sun* newspaper and they accepted it for publication, paying her twenty dollars. This article told about the decline in the shad fishery of the Chesapeake Estuary. It appeared March 1, 1936, and was just the beginning of a long working relationship with the *Baltimore Sun* and many other newspapers and magazines.

Elmer Higgins was so impressed with Rachel Carson's work on the radio scripts that he hired her

in July 1936 as a full-time junior aquatic biologist. In this government position, she was to continue with her writing duties, producing all kinds of informational brochures and reports. Most often she edited the research reports produced by the scientists at the U.S Bureau of Fisheries. She stayed in her government job until the early 1950s.

Undersea

Elmer Higgins, early on, had assigned Carson to write a brochure introducing a variety of little-known marine life to the American public. She completed writing the text for this brochure in April 1936 and met with Higgins to review the first draft.

Higgins found the work far too literary for a government brochure, but thought that one of the best literary magazines in the country would be interested in publishing it. Carson remembered later how "[m]y chief [Elmer Higgins] . . . handed it [the text] back with a twinkle in his eye. 'I don't think it will do,' he said. 'Better try again. But send this one to the *Atlantic.*'"[1]

Carson wrote a simpler, less poetic and literary version of the brochure, but she also immediately went to work turning the first draft of her piece into "Undersea," a long article that she wanted to send to *The Atlantic Monthly.*

Coral reef with tropical fish.

Despite her new full-time government job, Carson's family needed money more than ever. In January 1937, Marian died at the age of forty. Rachel Carson and her mother took over the care of Marian's two children, Virginia, age twelve, and Marjorie, age eleven.

In July, the Carson family got wonderful news: *The Atlantic Monthly* had read and loved Carson's piece and was going to publish it. The opening words of "Undersea" are as stirring today as they were more than seventy years ago when they were published in September 1937:

Who has known the ocean? Neither you nor I, with our earth-bound senses, know the foam and surge of the tide that beats over the crab hiding under the seaweed of his tide-pool home; or the lilt of the long, slow swells of mid-ocean, where shoals of wandering fish prey and are preyed upon, and the dolphin breaks the waves to breathe the upper atmosphere. Nor can we know the vicissitudes of life on the ocean floor, where the sunlight, filtering through a hundred feet of water, makes but a fleeting, bluish twilight, in which dwell sponge and mollusk and starfish and coral, where swarms of diminutive fish twinkle through the dusk like a silver rain of meteors, and eels lie in wait among the rocks. Even less is it given to man to descend those six incomprehensible miles into the recesses of the abyss, where reign utter silence and unvarying cold and eternal night.

To sense this world of waters known to the creatures of the sea we must shed our human perceptions of length and breadth and time and place, and enter vicariously into a universe of all-pervading water. For to the sea's children nothing is so important as the fluidity of their world. It is water that they breathe; water that brings them food; water through which they see, by filtered sunshine from which first the red rays, then the greens, and finally the purples have been strained; water through which they sense vibrations equivalent to sound.[2]

With these words, and the poetically lyrical but scientifically precise paragraphs that followed, Rachel Carson launched her literary career. Though she had never traveled under the sea herself, her imagination took both her and her readers there. Her deep knowledge of biology allowed her to provide an illuminating view of the secret undersea world. She captivated readers in much the same way as Jules Verne had done in the 1800s with his work of fiction, *20,000 Leagues Under the Sea.* Carson's writing brought sea creatures alive and turned the blank slate of the ocean surface into a canvas brimming with adventure.

The Start of a Shining Career

Rachel Carson's piece for *The Atlantic Monthly* caught the eye of two key people. It was spotted by Quincy Howe, the editor for Simon and Schuster books. Howe wrote Carson a letter proposing that

she write a book about the world under the sea. Well-known journalist Willem van Loon, author of a best-selling book in the 1920s called *The Story of Mankind,* also wrote to Carson praising her work. Howe and van Loon put their heads together immediately, discussing the possibility for Carson's first book, and made plans to meet this aspiring young writer. The three met in January 1938, and within days, Carson began sketching out an outline for the book that would become *Under the Sea-Wind.*

At first, Carson thought that her book should feature a variety of protagonists: birds, fish, and sea-going mammals that would tell her story. But more and more she recognized that the main character of her first book would be the sea itself. The book would describe the sea in all of its moods, from peaceful to stormy, and in all of its habitats, from the river mouth, to the tidal beaches, to the largely unexplored fathomless depths.

The Difficult Job of Writing

Rachel Carson found that finding the time to write wasn't easy. She still had to hold down her day job with the U.S. Bureau of Fisheries. And though her mother did most of the household chores, Carson still needed to keep up with her own duties as head of the family. In addition to working full-time, she continued to write magazine and newspaper articles in her off hours. She worked

Rachel Carson's government photograph taken while she was working for the United States Fish and Wildlife Service in 1944.

on her first book late into the night, with only her cats as companions. She wrote to a friend:

> In those concluding months of work on the book (fall of 1940) I often wrote late at night. . . . My constant companions during those otherwise solitary sessions were two precious Persian cats, Buzzie and Kito. Buzzie in particular used to sleep on my writing table, on the litter of notes and manuscript sheets. On two of these pages I had made sketches, first of his little head drooping with sleepiness, then of him after he had settled down comfortably for a nap.[3]

Rachel Carson was a slow writer who took painstaking care with the selection of each word. She would sometimes rewrite one sentence or paragraph many times over before being satisfied and moving on to the next. She often read sections of the book aloud to make sure its rhythms perfectly evoked the sea. And not satisfied with that, she would have her mother read chapters back to her aloud in order to be sure that every word was pulling its weight and reaching its audience.

Under the Sea-Wind

Carson finished her first book on schedule, meeting her deadline of December 31, 1940. Those who had read "Undersea," her article in *The Atlantic Monthly,* were not disappointed by *Under the Sea-Wind.* The book chronicles the life cycles of fish

and birds as they travel their mysterious migratory routes. Here, for example, Carson captures migratory life among the fish beneath the waves:

> The spring sea was filled with hurrying fishes. Scup were migrating northward from their wintering grounds off the Capes of Virginia, bound for the coastal waters of southern New England where they would spawn. Shoals of young herring moved swiftly just under the surface, rippling the water no more than the passing of a breeze, and schools of menhaden, moving in closely packed formation with bodies flashing bronze and silver in the sun, appeared to the watching sea birds like dark clouds ruffling to a deep blue the smooth sheet of the sea. Mingled with the wandering menhaden and herring were late-running shad, following in along the sea lanes that led to the rivers of their birth, and across the silvery warp of this lifting fabric the last of the mackerel wove threads of flashing blue and green.[4]

And here Carson speculates on the migratory routes of one of the ocean's most mysterious creatures, the eel:

> The record of the eels' journey to their spawning place is hidden in the deep sea. No one can trace the path of the eels that left the salt marsh at the mouth of the bay on that November night when wind and tide brought them the feeling of warm ocean water—how they passed from the bay to the deep Atlantic basin that lies south of Bermuda and east of Florida half a thousand miles. Nor is there

a clearer record of the journey of those other eel hordes that in autumn passed to the sea from almost every river and stream of the whole Atlantic Coast from Greenland to Central America.[5]

Notice how Carson's writing evokes "the deep Atlantic basin," but it completely avoids anthropomorphism. She never gives the fish and animals she writes about human characteristics. Instead, she sees them as creatures existing in their own right, in their own undersea world.

Reviewers at *The New York Times,* the *New York Herald Tribune, The New Yorker, The Christian Science Monitor,* and the *Chicago Tribune* praised Carson's new book. *The New York Times Book Review* praised *Under the Sea-Wind,* saying that Carson's "drama of ocean life unfolds with charm and lucidity. The audience will leave this fabled theatre [of the sea] with a sense of enrichment."[6]

Scientists too loved the book. Renowned oceanographer and bathysphere inventor William Beebe was one of these scientists. He chose to include two chapters of Carson's book in an anthology of the best natural history writing.

Despite the quality of the writing and the wildly positive reviews, *Under the Sea-Wind* was doomed to failure by events beyond anyone's control. Only a month after the book appeared in print, the Japanese attacked Pearl Harbor in the Hawaiian Islands, bringing the United States into

World War II. As a result, the book received little notice, and its publication was swallowed up in the bad war news from Europe and the Pacific. *Under the Sea-Wind* sold just 1,348 copies in its first year, and six years later its total sales still hovered around a mere 1,600 copies. Carson's total royalties for the book when it went out of print in 1946 were $689.17. She bought the remaining copies from the publisher and gave them as gifts to friends.

Carson was disappointed in the book's sales, especially since she had hoped that it would help her family get out of financial trouble. Instead, she found that she could make more money laboring over magazine articles late into the night than she could from her book writing.

Continued Promotion Within the Government

Fortunately, Rachel Carson's hard work and gifts as a scientist earned her regular promotions in her government job. In 1940, the Bureau of Fisheries (part of the Department of Commerce) was merged with the Biological Survey in the Department of Agriculture, becoming the U.S. Fish and Wildlife Service. It was administered by the Department of the Interior. Carson worked diligently during the war years, rising from junior aquatic biologist, to assistant aquatic biologist (1942–1943), then

associate aquatic biologist (1943–1945), and finally to full aquatic biologist (1945–1946).

From 1946 to 1949, Carson worked as information specialist to the Fish and Wildlife Service. In 1949, she rose to editor in chief of the Information Division of the U.S. Fish and Wildlife Service, a position she held until she left the service in 1951 to pursue her literary career.

Achieving Fame

Rachel Carson wasn't one to give up too easily. Even after the failure of her first book, she continued to write for magazines and newspapers. During World War II, for example, she used recently declassified military secrets to create new nature articles. One of these pieces, published in *Collier's* magazine in 1945 and called "The Bat Knew It First," explained echolocation—a system used to locate objects by sound waves reflected back. Bats give off high-pitched sounds, then interpret the echoes to navigate and find food. This same piece was reprinted in *Reader's Digest,* a popular periodical. Carson received five hundred dollars for her

story from *Reader's Digest,* a good sum of money in those days. Carson's magazine and newspaper writing provided much needed income to her family. The bat article was also noticed by the U.S. Navy, which thought it one of the best explanations of the working of radar ever written. The navy made the article required reading for its radar operators.

Rachel Carson was slowly carving a niche for herself as a popular science writer who could make complex topics interesting and understandable to the average reader.

Conservation in Action

From 1946 to 1947, Rachel Carson had little time to write magazine articles. Instead, her job required her to write a series of brochures about the National Wildlife Refuge system, a series called *Conservation in Action.* In these brochures, she began to hone her message carefully about the importance of wildlife protection and the ecological interconnectedness of all life, themes that would be important to her later books. In the introduction to one brochure she wrote:

> The Western Hemisphere has a relatively short history of the exploitation of its natural resources by man. This history, though short, contains many chapters of reckless waste and appalling destruction. Entire species of animals have been exterminated,

CONSERVATION IN ACTION

GUARDING OUR
WILDLIFE
RESOURCES

Number FIVE

Fish and Wildlife Service, United States Department of the Interior, Washington, D. C.

As a marine biologist and editor for the U.S. Fish and Wildlife Service, Carson wrote and edited booklets, including this one, about the National Wildlife Refuge.

or reduced to so small a remnant that their survival is doubtful. Forests have been despoiled by uncontrolled and excessive cutting of lumber, grasslands have been destroyed by overgrazing. These and other practices have afflicted us with all the evils of soil erosion, floods, destruction of agricultural lands, and loss of wildlife habitats. . . .

But for all the people, the preservation of wildlife and of wildlife habitat means also the preservation of the basic resources of the earth, which men, as well as animals, must have in order to live. Wildlife, water, forests, grasslands—all are parts of man's essential environment; the conservation and effective use of one is impossible except as the others also are conserved.[1]

Carson's work for the U.S. Fish and Wildlife Service was so well received that in 1948 she was named editor in chief of the Fish and Wildlife Information Division. In that position she ran a small publishing business.

The Sea Around Us

During and after World War II, oceanographic researchers learned many new things about the world's oceans. Much of this information crossed Rachel Carson's desk as part of her job with the U.S. Fish and Wildlife Service. As more new studies and research piled up in her files, she decided to tackle the writing of a second natural history book that would reveal much of this new information to

While working for the government and writing the book, *The Sea Around Us,* Carson spent ten days and nights at sea on this U.S. Fish and Wildlife Service ship, the Albatross III.

the public. In 1948, Carson wrote to the famous oceanographer William Beebe that "the book I am writing is something I have had in mind for a good while. I have had to wait to undertake it until at least a part of the wartime oceanic studies should be published."[2]

Carson had little time to write, though, given her full-time government job and heavy family responsibilities. She could only manage to write for

herself late at night or early in the morning. In 1949, a Eugene F. Saxton Memorial Fellowship freed her to work on the book that she now tentatively called *The Sea Around Us.*

As part of her research, Rachel Carson went to Florida and took her first and only dive below the ocean's surface. She also sailed on the *Albatross III,* a research vessel, and watched as its sonar mapped the contours of the ocean floor.

The result of all this was a book that brought Rachel Carson from relative obscurity to fame. *The New Yorker* magazine offered her the equivalent of a year's salary in her government job to publish excerpted chapters from the book. And in 1951, the *Yale Review* published the chapter, "The Birth of an Island," which won Carson a one thousand dollar George Westinghouse Science Writing Award. With such intense prepublication publicity, sales of the book soared when it finally appeared in print in 1951, making it a best seller and Rachel Carson famous.

In *The Sea Around Us,* Carson explores the origins of the world's oceans and the beginnings of life within their "primordial soup." She draws dramatic connections between sea life and all life. She wrote:

> Each of us carries in our veins a salty stream in which the elements sodium, potassium, and calcium are combined in almost the same proportions

as in sea water. This is our inheritance from the day, untold millions of years ago, when a remote ancestor, having progressed from the one-cellular to the many-cellular stage, first developed a circulatory system in which the fluid was merely the water of the sea.[3]

The Sea Around Us won the National Book Award for the best nonfiction book

RACHEL L. CARSON

THE SEA AROUND US

Revised edition with illustrations

⬆ Book jacket of *The Sea Around Us.*

of 1951. With that, Carson's publisher decided to put her first book, *Under the Sea-Wind* back into print. It too joined *The Sea Around Us* on the list of best sellers.

The Edge of the Sea

The success of *The Sea Around Us* allowed Carson to leave her job with the U.S. Fish and Wildlife Service and pursue a full-time writing career. It also led directly to Carson's third book, *The Edge of the Sea*. This book is a personal narrative that

uses Carson as the observer. It serves as a lyrically written field guide to the flora and fauna of the North American coast.

In its pages we hear echoes of the innocent writings of her youth, such as "My Favorite Recreation," when she wrote about exploring the Pennsylvania

hills with her dog, Pal. Carson's writing in *The Edge of the Sea* is so compelling, so alive with word pictures, that we cannot help but be drawn from the shore into the tide pools and the crashing waves of the mysterious coast.

Cleared land on Ohio Key, with a section of the overseas highway in the background. On the other side of the road, land has been cleared to make room for a "Travel-Trailer" camp. This small key has changed significantly in the years since Rachel Carson camped here to do research for her book, *The Edge of the Sea*. This photo was taken on June 6, 1973.

Sea stars, anemones, and barnacles, on a rock in a tidepool at Kalaloch Beach in Olympic National Park, Washington.

In my thoughts of the shore, one place stands apart for its revelation of exquisite beauty. It is a pool hidden within a cave that one can visit only rarely and briefly when the lowest of the year's low tides fall below it, and perhaps from that very fact it acquires some of its special beauty. Choosing such a tide, I hoped for a glimpse of the pool. . . .

And so I knelt on the wet carpet of sea moss and looked back into the dark cavern that held the pool in a shallow basin. The floor of the cave was only a few inches below the roof, and a mirror had been created in which all that grew on the ceiling was reflected in the still water below.

Under water that was clear as glass the pool was carpeted with green sponge. Gray patches of sea squirts glistened on the ceiling and colonies of soft coral were a pale apricot color. In the moment when I looked into the cave a little elfin starfish hung down, suspended by the merest thread, perhaps by only a single tube foot. It reached down to touch its own reflection, so perfectly delineated that there might have been, not one starfish, but two. The beauty of the reflected images and of the limpid pool itself was the poignant beauty of things that are ephemeral, existing only until the sea should return to fill the little cave.[4]

The Edge of the Sea was another best seller, and with it Rachel Carson achieved fame as a lyrical writer about science for the common man. She, along with writers like forester and ecologist

Aldo Leopold, helped invent the modern literary genre of environmental natural history.

Success and Sadness

As Carson became well known, and her financial worries became less severe, a series of sad events darkened her life. First, Mary Scott Skinker, her close friend and mentor from her college years and after, passed away. Skinker died of cancer in December 1948.

Carson's niece Marjorie died in 1957. Carson had been very fond of her and was saddened by the loss. Carson and her ninety-year-old mother decided to take in Marjorie's six-year-old son Roger Christie.

The worst blow came in November 1958, when her mother, with whom she had lived almost her entire life, passed away. In a letter to her close friend Dorothy Freeman, Carson talked about the last moments she spent with her mother, and how she found solace and peace in nature when her mother died.

> During that last agonizing night, I sat most of the time by the bed with my hand slipped under the border of the oxygen tent, holding Mamma's [hand]. Of course I didn't feel she knew, and occasionally I slipped away into the dark living room, to look out of the picture window at the trees and the sky. . . . [The constellation of] Orion stood in all his glory just above the horizon of our woods,

and several other stars blazed more highly than I can remember ever seeing them. Then I went back into the room and at 6:05 she slipped away, her hand in mine. I told [nephew] Roger about the stars just before Grandma left us, and he said, "Maybe they were the lights of the angels, coming to take her to heaven."[5]

Unfortunately, Rachel Carson would not have her most influential mentor, her beloved mother, at her side as she wrote her most important book, *Silent Spring.*

6

Silent Spring

Reading Rachel Carson's first three books, no one would have guessed that her fourth would become one of the most controversial and influential books in American history. Critics have favorably compared its trailblazing importance to Thomas Paine's *Common Sense,* which helped launch the American Revolution; Harriet Beecher Stowe's *Uncle Tom's Cabin,* which helped end slavery in the United States; and Upton Sinclair's *The Jungle,* which led to the regulation of the meat-packing industry in the early twentieth century.

Silent Spring, released in 1962, warned the world that the uncontrolled use of synthetic

chemical pesticides was devastating ecosystems and threatening human health.

But *Silent Spring* did more than just indict the use of DDT and other chemical pesticides. Carson challenged the whole notion of progress. She doubted that every industrial development was necessarily good for humanity and good for nature. For the first time, a citizen and beneficiary of all the positive things that industry had produced, came forward to question the entire assumption of progress.

Carson asked whether our determination to control nature wasn't in fact a war against all living things and against ourselves. Was not this shower of toxic chemicals unbalancing nature and changing the environment for the worse in terrible and unexpected ways? For this very reason, *Silent Spring* was a pioneering work, and a work that

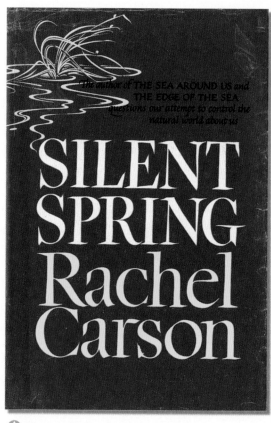

the author of THE SEA AROUND US and THE EDGE OF THE SEA questions our attempt to control the natural world about us

SILENT SPRING Rachel Carson

⊙ Book jacket of *Silent Spring*.

influenced the entire shape of the then-evolving environmental movement.

First Concerns About DDT

Rachel Carson first became aware of the possible dangers of DDT in 1945. She told the *Reader's Digest* editors about recent testing by U.S. Fish and Wildlife biologists at the Patuxent Research Refuge in Maryland of DDT, a much-heralded "miracle" pesticide.

DDT, short for **d**ichloro-**d**iphenyl-**t**richloroethane, had saved possibly millions of lives during World War II by combating malaria, typhus, and other insect-borne human diseases among both soldiers and civilian populations.

Though DDT had been declared a miracle pesticide, and though it came into wide agricultural and commercial usage in this country in the late 1940s, the Patuxent scientists had found something disturbing. Their research showed that DDT not only killed pest insects, but beneficial ones as well. They also found indications that DDT might be harming waterfowl and other birds that ate DDT-loaded insects.

In her query letter to *Reader's Digest,* Carson wrote: "The experiments at Patuxent have been planned to show what effects DDT may have if applied to wide areas: what it will do to insects that are beneficial or even essential: how it may

affect waterfowl, or birds that depend on insect food; whether it may upset the whole delicate balance of nature if unwisely used."[1]

In 1945, *Reader's Digest* was more concerned about another scientific miracle, the atomic bomb, than it was about possible side effects of DDT.

Pesticide Production Explodes

DDT was originally synthesized in 1874, but its insecticidal capabilities weren't discovered until 1939, on the eve of World War II. Insect pests had long inflicted deadly diseases on soldiers. The U.S. armed forces used DDT very successfully to protect its troops from disease.

So successful was DDT in controlling pests that in 1948 Swiss chemist Paul Hermann Müller was awarded the Nobel Prize in Physiology or Medicine "for his discovery of the high efficiency of DDT as a contact poison against several arthropods."[2]

In his award acceptance speech, Müller praised the use of DDT against the lice that transmit the disease typhus:

> The war situation demanded speedy action. DDT was manufactured on a vast scale whilst a series of experiments determined methods of application. Particularly energetic was General Fox, Physician-in-Chief to the American forces.

In October of 1943 a heavy outbreak of typhus occurred in Naples [Italy] and the customary relief measures proved totally inadequate. General Fox thereupon introduced DDT treatment with total exclusion of the old, slow methods of treatment. As a result, 1,300,000 people were treated in January 1944 and in a period of three weeks the typhus epidemic was completely mastered. Thus, for the first time in history a typhus outbreak was brought under control in winter.[3]

Chemical manufacturers saw that synthetic pesticides like DDT could be a gold mine for them, leading to huge profits. After World War II, DDT was made available not just for controlling insect-borne diseases, but for use as an agricultural insecticide. Soon its production and use skyrocketed, along with more potent insecticides and herbicides.

From 1942 until its ban in 1972, about 675,000 tons of DDT were applied domestically. The peak year for use in the United States was 1959 when nearly 80 million pounds were applied to trees, shrubs, and crops. From that high point, usage declined steadily to about 13 million pounds in 1971, most of it applied to cotton. This decline in usage was caused not only by the introduction of other more efficient pesticides, but also because insects began to build up a resistance to DDT; the chemical no longer controlled them effectively.

The pesticide dichloro-diphenyl-trichloroethane (DDT) at first seemed like a miracle chemical. It was very effective at killing many kind of insects, including disease-carrying lice and mosquitoes. Here a woman in Linz, Austria is dusted with DDT powder to kill lice in 1945.

Unfortunately, what no one realized was that the miracle insecticide DDT was an indiscriminate killer, that it could take the lives of pest and beneficial insects, wildlife, and even human beings.

A Growing Concern

In 1958, Olga Huckins, a journalist and friend of Rachel Carson, sent Rachel a letter that helped spur Carson into action on her book *Silent Spring*. Huckins complained about Massachusetts aerial spraying of DDT to control mosquitoes. She wrote:

> The "harmless" shower bath [of DDT] killed seven of our lovely songbirds outright. We picked up three dead bodies the next morning right by the door. . . . The next day three were scattered around the bird bath. I had emptied it and scrubbed it after the spraying but YOU CAN NEVER KILL DDT. On the following day one robin dropped suddenly from a branch in our woods. We were too heartsick to hunt for other corpses. All of these birds died horribly, and in the same way. Their bills were gaping open, and their splayed claws drawn up to breasts in agony.[4]

The letter reached Carson at a time when some scientists began to doubt that DDT was safe for widespread use. As Carson began her research, she found evidence that in areas sprayed by DDT, baby birds were not hatching, or they were born grossly malformed. Some fertilized eggs weren't developing into chicks at all. Bird populations

A pesticide spraying program in a coastal area of Duxbury, Massachusetts, killed songbirds and outraged property owners.

were falling, and Carson thought she knew why. DDT was the cause.

Her book research showed that the poison was working in several ways. It not only killed birds when large amounts of it were sprayed, as Huckins had noted. Worse, DDT was a persistent pesticide, meaning that it stayed in the environment for a long time without breaking down into harmless chemicals. In that way, DDT entered the food chain. Insects were eaten by birds, and the more DDT-contaminated insects the birds ate, the more poison entered their systems. Even if DDT wasn't enough to kill a mother bird, it could cause harm to her offspring. One of the birds most affected was the American eagle, symbol of the United States, which was threatened with extinction by the use of DDT.

Carson believed that DDT and other insecticides were poisoning the entire food chain, contaminating creatures small and large, from the tiniest insects to birds and fish to mammals and human beings. In a letter to her editor at Houghton Mifflin Publishing Company, she wrote: "I shall be able to support a claim to even more serious and insidious effects [of pesticides], which include the most basic functions of every living cell. . . . I shall be able to show that the chemicals used as insecticides interfere with many of the

enzymes that control the most basic functions of the body."[5]

Writing *Silent Spring*

It took four years for Rachel Carson to research and write *Silent Spring*. These were difficult years for her personally. As she started work on the book in 1958, her lifetime mentor, her mother, died. And just two years later, Rachel was diagnosed with breast cancer, and she underwent painful and exhausting surgery. Though in pain and fatigued, Rachel diligently gathered more data and wrote her book.

This book would be different from the previous ones she had written. In her sea books, Carson had celebrated life and nature. In *Silent Spring,* she came to the defense of nature. She did more than make the case against the chemical pesticide industry. She made a case against uncontrolled human "progress."

Up to that time, almost all new human inventions had been seen as good, and nature was seen as a servant to humankind. Carson was among the first to recognize, and make the case scientifically, that not all progress and development were good. Though she recognized the benefits of pesticides when properly used, she also recognized that their careless and irresponsible use was a threat to all living things. At the end of *Silent Spring* she wrote:

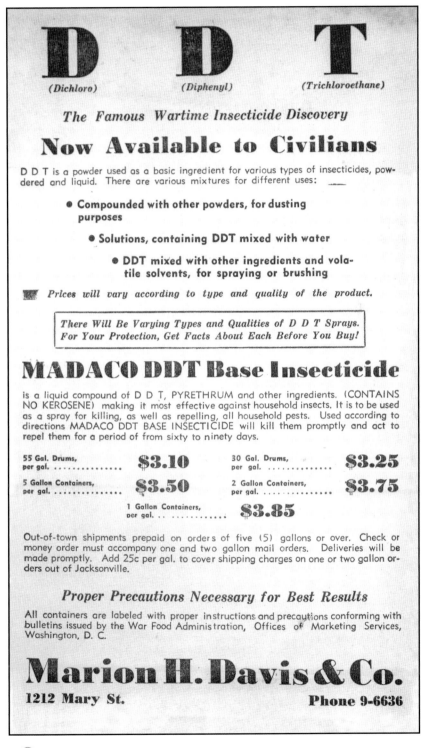

An advertisement in the *Tallahassee Democrat* newspaper announcing DDT for sale to the public.

The "control of nature" is a phrase conceived in arrogance, born of the Neanderthal age of biology and philosophy, when it was supposed that nature exists for the convenience of man. . . . It is our alarming misfortune that so primitive a science has armed itself with the most modern and terrible [chemical pesticide] weapons, and that in turning them against the insects it has also turned them against the earth.[6]

The Chemical Industry Fights Back

The publication of parts of *Silent Spring* in *The New Yorker* magazine, beginning on June 16, 1962, created what *The New York Times* called a "Noisy Summer." Scientists and Carson supporters in government rushed to her defense. Meanwhile, the chemical industry and some officials in government launched a relentless attack on the book and on Carson herself. At the time of the book's release, *The New York Times* reported:

The $300,000,000 pesticides industry has been highly irritated by a quiet woman author whose previous works on science have been praised for the beauty and precision of the writing. . . .

In her latest work, however, Miss Carson is not so gentle. More pointed than poetic, she argues that the widespread use of pesticides is dangerously tilting the so-called balance of nature. Pesticides poison not only pests, she says, but also humans, wildlife, the soil, food and water.

The Quiet Crisis

⬆ United States Secretary of the Interior Stuart Udall presents an award to Rachel Carson in 1962.

The men who make the pesticides are crying foul. "Crass commercialism or idealistic flag waving," scoffs one industrial toxicologist. "We are aghast," says another. "Our members are raising hell;" reports a trade association.

The president of the Montrose Chemical Corporation of California, the largest maker of DDT, said that Carson wrote "not as a scientist but rather as a fanatic defender of the cult of the balance of nature."[7]

The chemical industry mobilized against Rachel Carson. The National Agricultural Chemicals Association, a trade group of the pesticide industry, spent more than $250,000 (that's equivalent to $1.4 million today) to attack Carson's book. One chemical company threatened to sue Houghton Mifflin, the publisher of *Silent Spring*, *The New Yorker,* and *Audubon* magazine, which had published parts of the book. But no lawsuits came.

Despite these attacks or even because of them, *Silent Spring* jumped to the best seller list.

A Book That Changed History

By the end of 1962, there were more than forty bills in state legislatures set up to regulate pesticides. President John F. Kennedy ordered his Science Advisory Committee to look at *Silent Spring* and either confirm or refute the facts of the

book. In 1963, the committee supported Carson's findings in *Silent Spring* and vindicated her.

On April 3, 1963, the Columbia Broadcasting System's television series *CBS Reports* presented the program "The Silent Spring of Rachel Carson." In it, Rachel Carson spoke her mind in a statement that has reverberated through the environmental movement over the past half-century. She said:

> It is the public that is being asked to assume the risks that the insect controllers calculate. The public must decide whether it wishes to continue on the present road, and it can do so only when in full possession of the facts. We still talk in terms of conquest. We still haven't become mature enough to think of ourselves as only a tiny part of a vast and incredible universe. Man's attitude toward nature is today critically important simply because we have now acquired a fateful power to alter and destroy nature. But man is a part of nature, and his war against nature is inevitably a war against himself. The rains have become an instrument to bring down from the atmosphere the deadly products of atomic explosions. Water, which is probably our most important natural resource, is now used and re-used with incredible recklessness. Now, I truly believe, that we in this generation, must come to terms with nature, and I think we're challenged as mankind has never been challenged before to prove our maturity and our mastery, not of nature, but of ourselves.[8]

The struggle to live peacefully and coopera-
tively with nature continues today. Unfortunately,
Rachel Carson didn't live to see the triumphs of
the environmental movement that she inspired.
On April 14, 1964, she died of heart failure after a
long battle with breast cancer. Her friends spread
half her ashes along the rocky coast of Maine, a
beloved spot where she had come to vacation for
many years; the other half of her ashes were
buried next to her mother in Silver Spring.

7

Rachel Carson's Legacy

In 1972, just ten years after *Silent Spring* was published and eight years after Rachel Carson's death, the U.S. Environmental Protection Agency (EPA) banned the use of DDT in the United States. The EPA press release reads in part: "The general use of the pesticide DDT will no longer be legal in the United States after today [December, 31, 1972], ending nearly three decades of application during which time the once-popular chemical was used to control insect pests on crop and forest lands, around homes and gardens, and for industrial and commercial purposes."[1]

⬆ Rachel Carson's book *Silent Spring* alerted readers to the dangers of DDT and other pesticides. Since the ban on DDT, many species have made impressive recoveries. These healthy bald eagle chicks will likely live healthier, longer lives thanks to Rachel Carson's writing.

It is likely that the banning of DDT saved the American bald eagle, our national symbol, from extinction—along with a variety of other endangered species. However, DDT use was never banned outside the United States, and some countries continue to use the pesticide to control mosquitoes and other insect pests today.

Pioneer of the Environmental Movement

Though Rachel Carson died in 1964, her words and legacy live on and have shaped the environmental movement.

Time magazine counted Carson among the one hundred most important people of the twentieth century. Writing in *Time,* nature writer Peter Matthiessen said:

> *Silent Spring* became a runaway best seller, with international reverberations. . . . [I]t is still regarded as the cornerstone of the new environmentalism. Carson was not a born crusader but an intelligent and dedicated woman who rose heroically to the occasion. She was rightly confident about her facts as well as her ability to present them. . . .
>
> True, the damage being done by poison chemicals today is far worse than it was when she wrote the book. Yet one shudders to imagine how much more impoverished our habitat would be had

Silent Spring not sounded the alarm. Well crafted, fearless and succinct, it remains her most celebrated book, although her wonderful essays on the sea may be remembered longer. Even if she had not inspired a generation of activists, Carson would prevail as one of the greatest nature writers in American letters.[2]

The Ecology Hall of Fame describes Carson's legacy:

Rachel Carson made environmentalism respectable. Before *Silent Spring,* nearly all Americans believed that science was a force for good. Carson's work exposed the dark side of science. It showed that DDT and other chemicals we were using to enhance agricultural productivity were poisoning our lakes, rivers, oceans, and ourselves. Thanks to her, progress can no longer be measured solely in tons of wheat produced and millions of insects killed. Thanks to her, the destruction of nature can no longer be called progress.[3]

Linda Lear, author of an authoritative biography on Carson, said of her, "Rachel Carson was about life. She cared about the whole of the living world."[4]

The Carson Controversy Continues

The year 2007 marked the one hundredth anniversary of Rachel Carson's birth. Maryland senator Ben Cardin introduced a resolution celebrating Rachel Carson's life, which states: "Congress honors

the life of Rachel Carson, a scientist, writer, and pioneer in the environmental movement, on the occasion of the centennial of her birth."[5] A bipartisan group of senators also cosponsored the resolution, including Barbara Boxer, a Democrat from California, the chairperson of the Senate Environment and Public Works Committee.

Although the woman credited with launching the modern environmental movement has been praised by many, some used the anniversary to make scathing and unfounded attacks.

Senator Tom Coburn, an Oklahoma Republican, and an opponent of environmental causes, single-handedly held up two Senate bills that would honor Rachel Carson and her book, *Silent Spring*. Coburn's spokesperson said, "Millions of people in the developing world, particularly children under five, died because governments bought into Carson's junk science claims about DDT. To put it in language the Left understands, her 'intelligence' was wrong and it had deadly consequences."[6]

Such claims as Coburn's have again and again proved false. In this case, he and others blame Carson for a worldwide DDT ban that doesn't even exist. Critics of Carson, such as right-wing Rush Limbaugh, a radio talk-show host, say that Rachel Carson caused thirty million human malaria deaths globally because of the ban of DDT. But the

fact of the matter is that DDT is still used to battle malarial mosquitoes in Third World countries, and that Rachel Carson never advocated for the pesticide's outright ban. She recognized the good done by many pesticides. She only suggested we look at their dangers along with their benefits, and then use the products judiciously.

Following in Rachel Carson's Footsteps

The problems caused by pesticides and other chemicals in the environment did not end with the publication of *Silent Spring* and the banning of DDT in the United States. In fact, the production of synthetic chemicals and new pesticides has soared. As many as eighty thousand new synthetic chemicals have been introduced into the environment, most of them since World War II, and most of them never tested for their harmful effects.

In 2003, the U.S. Center for Disease Control did a study of 9,282 Americans, looking for 116 chemicals in their bodies, including 34 pesticides. The study found that among those tested for pesticide residues, the average person had 13 pesticides in his or her body. The study also found especially high levels of dangerous pesticides in children's bodies.

There are many opportunities for young people to continue the work of Rachel Carson.

The Rachel Carson National Wildlife Refuge in Maine provides important feeding and breeding grounds for many species of migratory and shore birds. The refuge was established in 1966 and was renamed to honor Rachel Carson in 1969.

They can follow in Carson's footsteps by becoming environmental activists, environmental scientists, environmental writers, or even environmental lawyers. They can try to change environmental policies and write legislation controlling pesticide and chemical use.

See the World as Rachel Carson Saw It

There are many ways in which you can prepare for a career in environmental science. You can do what Rachel Carson did when she was a young girl. The very first step is to go for a walk and try to begin to see the world as Rachel Carson saw it. Leave your house and then look back at it and realize that everything in it—the walls, roof, furniture, appliances, toys, and books—all came from nature, and that some part of nature was affected so you could have these things.

Take a field guide and a magnifying glass with you on your walk. Look closely. No matter where you live you will find signs of nature. Everything around you—the largest trees, the smallest ants, the robins and the mosquitoes, the sky above and the soil beneath your feet—is part of your ecosystem. There is so much to learn. But it is all spread out before you, just as it was for Rachel Carson.

Ultimately, said Rachel Carson, only one thing is really needed to become a lover of nature and a

person who wants to protect it, and that is a sense of wonder. In her last book, *The Sense of Wonder,* Rachel Carson offers a message about children and their inborn sense of wonder:

> A child's world is fresh and new and beautiful, full of wonder and excitement. It is our misfortune that for most of us that clear-eyed vision, that true instinct for what is beautiful and awe-inspiring, is dimmed and even lost before we reach adulthood. If I had influence with the good fairy who is supposed to preside over the christening of all children I should ask that her gift to each child in the world be a sense of wonder so indestructible that it would last throughout life, as an unfailing antidote against the boredom and disenchantments of later years, the sterile preoccupation with things that are artificial, the alienation from the sources of our strength.[7]

A Lasting Legacy

There is no doubt that Rachel Carson will continue to be a controversial figure. Environmentalists will hold her up as a founder of their movement, but those who continue to view humans as having power over nature will continue to attack her. Carl Safina, founder and president of Blue Ocean Institute, offers this moving testimony to Carson:

> Rachel Carson was the best thing America is capable of producing: a modest person, concerned, courageous, and profoundly right—all at the same

time. Troubled by knowledge of an emerging threat to the web of life, she took pains to become informed, summoned her courage, breached her confines, and conveyed a diligently constructed message with eloquence enough to catalyze a new social movement. Her life addressed the promise and premise of being truly human.[8]

Careers in the Environment

Where to pursue a career in environmental science and activism:

National Institute of Environmental Health Sciences (NIEHS)—To find out what an epidemiologist does or talk to a microbiologist or wetland ecologist, check out the NIEHS Web site to begin your exploration of environmental science career possibilities. <http://kids.niehs.nih.gov/labcoat.htm>

Environmental Education for Kids (EEK!)—This Web site offers a kid friendly guide to environmental science, plus a page that tells about all kinds of environmental careers ranging from being a wildlife biologist to being a herpetologist. <http://www.dnr.state.wi.us/org/caer/ce/eek/job/index.htm>

Sea Grant Marine Careers—To find out how to be an oceanographer or marine biologist like Rachel Carson, go to this Web site to learn how you can pursue a career studying the world's oceans. <http://www.marinecareers.net>

National Nonprofit Environmental Organizations—Groups such as the Sierra Club hire environmental scientists and writers to provide information to the public about such topics as pesticides. There are hundreds of environmental groups in the United States. You can find national organizations listed on the Internet. <http://www.umt.edu/asum/envirolaw/nationalenvirolinks.htm>

Local Nonprofit Environmental Organizations—Check your phone book, library, or school to find out about groups dealing with local, regional, and state environmental issues. There are many places to learn about nature and to strive toward becoming an environmental scientist: local nature centers, natural history museums, arboretums, national, state, and local parks.

Natural Resources Defense Council Kids' Links—This Web site gives you links to all kinds of environmental topics, including sites that highlight animals, plants, habitats, oceans, global warming, and much more. <http://www.nrdc.org /reference/kids.asp>

Timeline

May 27, 1907—Rachel Carson is born in Springdale, Pennsylvania, to Robert and Maria Carson.

1918—Eleven-year-old Rachel receives ten dollars for her story "A Battle in the Clouds," published by *St. Nicholas Magazine.*

1925—Graduates from Parnassus High School and enters Pennsylvania College for Women (later named Chatham College).

1927—Changes her major from English to biology.

1929—Graduates from Pennsylvania College for Women; receives a summer fellowship to study at the Marine Biological Laboratory at Woods Hole, Massachusetts. She sees the ocean for the first time.

1932—Receives her master's degree in marine zoology from Johns Hopkins University.

1935—Begins her job with the U.S. Bureau of Fisheries by writing radio scripts.

1937—Carson's article "Undersea" is published in The Atlantic Monthly.

1941—Carson's first book, *Under the Sea-Wind,* is published. Though critically acclaimed, it sells poorly.

1945—Sends a query to Reader's Digest magazine suggesting a story about the hazards of pesticides.

1951—Carson's second book, *The Sea Around Us,* is published and becomes a best seller.

1955—Her third book, *The Edge of the Sea,* is published and also becomes a best seller.

1958—Carson begins work on *Silent Spring,* her book documenting the harm done to ecosystems by pesticides.

1962—*Silent Spring* is published, becomes a best seller and is attacked by the pesticides industry.

1963—President John F. Kennedy's Science Advisory Committee supports Rachel Carson's findings in Silent Spring.

April 14, 1964—Rachel Carson dies of breast cancer and heart failure.

1972—The chemical pesticide DDT is banned in the United States.

1980—Rachel Carson is awarded posthumously the Presidential Medal of Freedom.

2007—On the one hundredth anniversary of Rachel Carson's birth, some U.S. senators try to recognize her achievements. Anti-environmentalists block the effort.

Glossary

anthropomorphized—Writing or storytelling in which wildlife is given the characteristics of people, as opposed to a more scientific approach that portrays wildlife accurately in its natural habitat.

bathysphere—A hollow metal ball containing oxygen from which a diver can be lowered into the sea.

conservation—The care, protection and management of natural resources

DDT—Short for Dichloro-Diphenyl-Trichloroethane, one of the first pesticides.

echolocation— a process for locating distant or invisible objects (as prey) by sound waves reflected back to the emitter (as a bat) from the objects.

food chain—The path of food consumption of transferring energy from one organism to another.

gender bias—Favoritism shown to one sex over the other, usually referring to jobs.

Great Depression—A financially troubled time beginning in 1929, when many of the nation's banks failed and there was widespread unemployment.

marine zoology—The study of sea life.

mentor—A teacher who inspires his/her student.

oceanography—The study of the world's seas

parable—A story that is meant to teach a lesson.

pesticide—A chemical intended to kill pests such as insects.

pesticide resistance—The genetically acquired ability of an organism to survive a pesticide application at doses that once killed most individuals of the same species.

protagonist—The main character in a story.

species—A category of living things

Chapter Notes

Chapter 1. The Environmental Movement Is Born

1. Rachel Carson, *Silent Spring* (Boston: Houghton Mifflin Company, 1961), p. 2.

2. Ibid., p. 2.

3. Ibid., p. 2.

4. Ibid., p. 3.

5. Ibid., p. 3.

6. USINFO.STATE.GOV, "Rachel Carson," n.d., <http://usinfo.state.gov/products/pubs/carson/mcintosh.htm> (October 11, 2007).

7. Carson, p. xv.

Chapter 2. The Birth of an Environmentalist

1. Anna Botsford Comstock, *Handbook of Nature Study,* "The Teaching of Nature Study," Vail-Ballou Press, 1957, <http://ia331336.us.archive.org/0/items/handbookofnature002506mbp/handbookofnature002506mbp_djvu.txt> (October 11, 2007).

2. Linda Lear, *Rachel Carson: Witness for Nature* (New York: Henry Holt and Company, 1997), p. 17.

3. George A. Smathers Library, University of Florida Digital Collection, "St. Nicholas Magazine," February 13, 2009, <http://web.uflib.ufl.edu/ufdc/UFDC.aspx?s=nick&> (October 11, 2007).

4. Rachel Carson Homestead Association, "The Spring," Issue No. 35?Spring 2007, <rachelcarsonhomestead.org/Portals/0/Spring%2007ii%20newsletter.pdf> (October 11, 2007).

5. Paul Brooks, *The House of Life: Rachel Carson at Work* (Boston: Houghton Mifflin Company, 1972), p. 17.

6. Lear, p. 8.

Chapter 3. The Path to Science

1. Linda Lear, *Rachel Carson: Witness for Nature* (New York: Henry Holt and Company, 1997), p. 32.

2. Ibid., p. 34.

3. Bartleby.com, "Locksley Hall," n.d., <http://www.bartleby.com/42/636.html> (October 11, 2007).

4. MBL Biological Discovery in Woods Hole, "Discover the MBL," n.d., <http://www.mbl.edu/about/discovery/index.html> (October 11, 2007).

5. Johns Hopkins University, "A Brief History of Jhu," [publication/revision date?], <http://webapps.jhu.edu/jhuniverse/information_about_hopkins/about_jhu/a_brief_history_of_jhu/index.cfm> (October 11, 2007).

Chapter 4. Eloquent Advocate for the Sea

1. Linda Lear, *Rachel Carson: Witness for Nature* (New York: Henry Holt and Company, 1997), p. 81.

2. The encyclopedia of earth, "Undersea (historical)," Atlantic Monthly, 78 (September 1937), pp. 55–67, <http:// www.eoearth.org/article/Undersea_(historical)> (October 11, 2007).

3. Paul Brooks, *The House of Life: Rachel Carson at Work* (Boston: Houghton Mifflin Company, 1972), p. 33.

4. Rachel Carson, *Under the Sea-Wind* (New York: The New American Library, 1941), p. 66.

5. Ibid., p. 124.

6. Ibid., back cover.

Chapter 5. Achieving Fame

1. Rachel Carson, *Conservation in Action: Guarding Our Wildlife Resources* (Washington, D.C., Fish and Wildlife Service, United States Department of the Interior, Number 5, 1948), p. 1.

2. Mary A. McCay, *Rachel Carson* (New York: Twayne Publishers, 1993), p. 39.

3. Ibid., p. 41.

4. Rachel Carson, *The Edge of the Sea* (Boston: Houghton Mifflin Company, 1955), pp. 1?2.

5. Martha Freeman, ed., *Always, Rachel: The Letters of Rachel Carson and Dorothy Freeman, 1952–1964* (Boston: Beacon Press, 1995), p. 273.

Chapter 6. *Silent Spring*

1. Kathleen Dean Moore and Lisa H. Sideris, eds. *Rachel Carson: Legacy and Challenge* (Albany, NY: State University of New York Press, 2008), p.197.

2. Nobelprize.org "The Nobel Prize in Physiology or Medicine 1948," n.d., <http://nobelprize.org/nobel_prizes/medicine/laureates/1948/> (October 11, 2007).

3. Nobelprize.org. "Presentation Speech," n.d., <http://nobelprize.org/nobel_prizes/medicine/laureates/1948/press.html> (October 11, 2007).

4. Douglas Allchin, "Advisory Committee on Pesticides" November 15, 1996, <www1.umn.edu/ships/pesticides/background.htm> (May 7, 2009).

5. Patricia Byrnes, *Environmental Pioneers* (Minneapolis, Minn.: Oliver Press, 1988), p.106.

6. Rachel Carson, *Silent Spring* (Boston: Houghton Mifflin Company, 1961), p. 297.

7. Living on Earth, "Rachel Carson Remembered," [publication/revision date?], <http://www.loe.org/shows/segments.htm?programID=07-P13-0021&segmentID=1> (October 11, 2007).

8. Johnathan Norton Leonard, "Rachel Carson Dies of Cancer; 'Silent Spring' Author was 56," *New York Times*, April 15, 1964 <www.nytimes.com/books/97/10/05/reviews/carson-obit.html >
(May 7, 2009).

Chapter 7. Rachel Carson's Legacy

1. U.S. Environmental Protection Agency, "DDT Ban Takes Effect," December 31, 1972, <http://www.epa.gov/history/topics/ddt/01.htm> (May 7, 2009).

2. *Time* "The Time 100: The Most Important People of the Century," <http://www.time.com/time/time100/scientist/profile/carson03.html> (October 11, 2007).

3. Ecology Hall of Fame "Rachel Carson 1907–1964," January 18, 2002, <http://www.ecotopia.org/ehof/carson/> (October 11, 2007).

4. Post-gazette NOW News "Environmentalist Rachel Carson's Legacy remembered on Earth Day," April 23, 2006, <http://www.post-gazette.com/pg/06113/684423-85.stm> (October 11, 2007).

5. Michael Roston, therawstory, "Republican environmental critic blocks honors for Rachel Carson, author of *Silent Spring*," May 2007, <http://rawstory.com/news/2007/Senator_blocks_honors_for_Rachel_Carson_0522.html> (October 11,2007).

6. Ibid.

7. Carson, Rachel. *The Sense of Wonder* (Berkeley, Calif.: The Nature Company Classics, 1956, 1990), unnumbered.

8. Rachel Carson, *The Sea Around Us* (Oxford: Oxford University Press, 1950), p. xvi.

Selected Works by Rachel Carson

Carson, Rachel L. *The Edge of the Sea*. Boston: Houghton Mifflin Company, 1955.

————*The Sea Around Us*. New York: Oxford University Press, 1951.

————*The Sense of Wonder*. New York, Harper & Row, 1965.

————*Silent Spring*. Boston: Houghton Mifflin Company, 2002

————*Under the Sea-Wind*. New York: Oxford University Press, 1941.

Further Reading

Dudley, William, ed. *The Environment.* Farmington Hills, MI.: Greenhaven Press, 2006.

Kudlinski, Kathleen. *Rachel Carson: Pioneer of Ecology.* New York: Puffin Books, 1997.

Levine, Ellen. *Rachel Carson: A Twentieth-Century Life.* New York: Viking, 2007.

Locker, Thomas. *Rachel Carson: Preserving a Sense of Wonder.* New York: Fulcurm Pub., 2004

Quaratiello, Arlene R. *Rachel Carson: A Biography.* Westport, Conn.: Greenwood Press, 2004.

Tremblay, E. A. and Sideman, Jill. *Rachel Carson: Author/Ecologist.* Broomall, Pa: Chelsea House Publishers, 2003.

Internet Addresses

The Rachel Carson Homestead
<http://www.rachelcarsonhomestead.org>

The Rachel Carson National Wildlife Refuge
<http://rachelcarson.fws.gov>

Index

J 92 CARSON
Fletcher, Marty.
Who on Earth is Rachel Carson? :

BN JBIO L8739374 c2009.